Woodworking
Mastering the Essentials of Craftsmanship
Basics

Woodworking

Mastering the Essentials of Craftsmanship

Basics

PETER KORN

The Taunton Press
Inspiration for hands-on living®

The Taunton Press, Inc., 63 South Main Street, PO Box 5506, Newtown, CT 06470-5506
e-mail: tp@taunton.com

EDITOR: Peter Chapman
JACKET/COVER DESIGN: Susan Fazekas
INTERIOR DESIGN AND LAYOUT: Susan Fazekas
ILLUSTRATOR: Peter Korn
PHOTOGRAPHER: Jim Dugan, except where noted

Library of Congress Cataloging-in-Publication Data
Korn, Peter, 1951-
    Woodworking basics : mastering the essentials of craftsmanship / Peter
Korn.
        p. cm.
    ISBN-13: 978-1-56158-620-2
    ISBN-10: 1-56158-620-X
  1. Woodwork--Amateurs' manuals. I. Title.
    TT185 .K69 2003
    684'.08--dc21

2003005043

Printed in the United States of America
10 9 8 7 6

The following manufacturers/names appearing in *Woodworking Basics* are trademarks: Lie-Nielson
Toolworks™, Lufkin®, Prismacolor pencil™, Sandvik®, Scotch-Brite®, Starrett®, Titlebond®, Ulmia™,
Waterlox® Original.

Working wood is inherently dangerous. Using hand or power tools improperly or ignoring safety practices
can lead to permanent injury or even death. Don't try to perform operations you learn about here (or
elsewhere) unless you're certain they are safe for you. If something about an operation doesn't feel right,
don't do it. Look for another way. We want you to enjoy the craft, so please keep safety foremost in your
mind whenever you're in the shop.

DEDICATION

To Kully Rohlen and Craig Satterlee,
generous spirits who have done
so much so quietly

ACKNOWLEDGMENTS

THE ORIGINAL VERSION of this book was published by The Taunton Press ten years ago, under the title *Working with Wood: The Basics of Craftsmanship*. In that same year, 1993, I started a small school in the barn behind my house in Rockland, Maine. I believe that the publication of the book was responsible for the early success of the school, and for that I remain grateful to my first publisher and editors: John Kelsey, Andy Schultz, and Peter Chapman.

As the years have progressed, the Center for Furniture Craftsmanship has become a far more vibrant and comprehensive school than I could ever have imagined in those early days. Fortunately, with all the work of growing and running a school, I continue to have the opportunity to teach the Basic Woodworking course on which this text is based. As the course has evolved over time, the need for a revised version of the text has grown. My thanks to executive editor Helen Albert for making this possible.

I owe a debt of gratitude to the founding and current Boards of Directors of the Center for Furniture Craftsmanship for their collective vision and the gift of their time, experience, and resources. They have not only made the school's success possible, they have also encouraged me to continue writing. They are: Helen Albert, Jim Bowers, John Dunnigan, Ray Gauvin, Mark Horowitz, Al Hume, Rick Kellogg, John McAlevey, Jerry Morton, the late Andy Rheault, Craig Satterlee, Karin Thomas, Sam Trippe, and John Tuton.

I would also like to thank the many furniture makers from whom I have had the privilege to learn and with whom I have had the pleasure of teaching over the past two decades and more. These include, but are certainly not limited to: Chris Becksvoort, Brian Boggs, Lynette Breton, Art Carpenter, Tom Caspar, Bob DeFuccio, Bob Flexner, John Fox, Tage Frid, Andrew Garton, Garrett Hack, Jim Krenov, Phil Lowe, Sam Maloof, Teri Masaschi, Harv Mastalir, John McAlevey, Alan Peters, Stephen Proctor, Michael Puryear, Mario Rodriguez, Tim Rousseau, Carter Sio, Craig Stevens, and Rod Wales.

So far as the production of this book is concerned, huge thanks go to photographer Jim Dugan for his patience, professionalism, and unflappable good nature. Likewise, it has been a pleasure to work once again with editor Peter Chapman.

Finally, my love and appreciation to Michelle Dee for sharing life's every day.

CONTENTS

INTRODUCTION

THIS BOOK EVOLVED from the Basic Woodworking workshop that I began teaching in 1981 and still teach to this day. Class participants range from absolute beginners to experienced woodworkers who are competent with machinery but still need to master the hand skills so essential to fine craftsmanship. Like the course, this book presents indispensable information on wood characteristics, joinery, and tools, and then leads you through a series of projects that build upon one another sequentially. We begin by milling a piece of wood foursquare and end with construction of a handsome side table that incorporates a drawer and a frame-and-panel door. These exercises have worked well for my students over the years. If you read this book and carefully work through the projects, you will establish a solid foundation in woodworking craftsmanship that

will enable you to build beautiful furniture with confidence.

Although I have taught graduate and undergraduate furniture design at a university and still give courses for intermediate and advanced furniture makers, Basic Woodworking continues to be my favorite teaching experience. The excitement with which beginners approach the most mundane skills revitalizes my own sense of wonder. We begin with nothing more tangible than intent and end with a sensitive, sometimes beautiful object that will be an intimate part of daily life. What comes in between is craftsmanship.

To understand craftsmanship, we must ask not only "What has been made?" and "How has this been made?" but also "Who made this and why?" Craftsmanship is a relationship between the maker and the process of creation. It is not simply a set of skills one acquires, like the ability to read or drive a car. More than anything, craftsmanship is a matter of attitude: why we choose to devote time to such a demanding endeavor, why we choose to make a certain object of a certain appearance, and how we go about it.

In this context, craftsmanship is first and foremost an expression of the human spirit. I choose to work as a craftsman because the process answers a need of my spirit; the object I make is the physical expression of the interaction between spirit and matter. How is this different than the work of the artist?

The artist is not concerned with the utility of the created object; the craftsman is. I care that a chair be comfortable, sturdy, and durable, that it look inviting to sit in, that its presence in a room be neither overbearing nor withdrawn. This care is implicit in every step of making the chair—in drawing up the plans, choosing the wood, maintaining my tools, milling the rough lumber to size, cutting the joinery, planing, scraping, sanding, and applying the finish.

Craftsmanship is both attitude and skills. This book offers a foundation in both. Individual character will determine the pace of your growth as a craftsman and the nature of your work. In return, the practice of craftsmanship will affect your character.

There is no one right way to do anything in woodworking. The right way is the way that works best for you, and what works best is a balance between the time something takes, the tools available,

the pleasure you seek in the process, and the quality of result you are looking for. In my shop I prefer hand tools over machinery for joining and smoothing surfaces; I like the quiet, the control, and the communication between my hand and the work. Time is not as important to me as it is in a commercial shop. My personal concerns are quality and joy.

The methods and explanations offered in this book are understandings I have arrived at through 30 years of practice. I offer them not as the truth, but as one truth, as a starting point for your own journey into craftsmanship. As you continue learning, you may seek out teachers who will provide deeper insight into many areas of expertise, but always remember that the most valuable teacher you will encounter is yourself. Practice is the most essential component to mastering craftsmanship. Learn from your mistakes and successes, and, above all, learn from your hands.

(Photo by Randy O'Rourke)

Wood

WOOD IS SPECIAL for the same reason that it is quirky—it is a natural material that comes from trees. Wind, sun, shade, soil, site, rainfall, and competition with neighbors are among the variables that make each tree unique in the color, density, grain pattern, and working characteristics of the lumber it yields. As we fashion wood into furniture, every board reveals an individual personality in response to our tools. Skilled craftsmanship begins with an understanding of the characteristics imparted to wood by biology and the vagaries of tree growth.

PHYSICAL PROPERTIES

The wood in a tree is composed of long cells that run through its trunk, limbs, and branches. Basically, these cells are made of cellulose, the same material from which household sponges are made, and bound together with an adhesive called lignin.

You might picture a piece of wood as a bundle of straws (cells) held together with glue (lignin). The fibrous straws are difficult to break across their length, but relatively easy to pry apart from each other.

CROSS SECTION OF A TREE

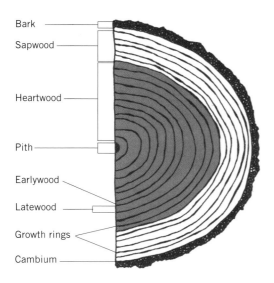

Bark
Sapwood
Heartwood
Pith
Earlywood
Latewood
Growth rings
Cambium

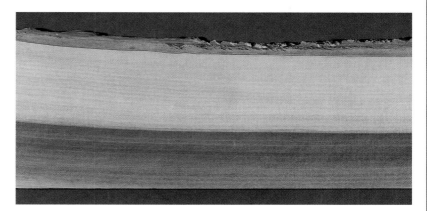

The change in color in this piece of yellow poplar clearly shows the division between heartwood and sapwood. (Photo by Randy O'Rourke)

This is why wood splits along the grain much more readily than across the grain.

A cross section of a living tree shows the different types of growth (see the drawing above). At the perimeter is the bark. The outer bark protects the tree from damage by insects, animals, the elements, and abrasion. The inner bark carries nutrients created by photosynthesis in the leaves to a thin layer of living growth cells—the cambium.

All tree growth takes place in the cambium; cells toward its outside become new bark, while cells toward its inside become new wood. Each year the cambium lays down a new outer ring of sapwood, which carries water from the root system to the canopy. As the inmost rings of sapwood lose their ability to carry sap upward, they stiffen and become heartwood,

COLOR IN DESIGN

When we think of walnut as a dark, richly colored wood, we are thinking of its heartwood. The sapwood of walnut, as of most hardwood species, is lighter in color and slightly softer. Woods such as walnut, cherry, and oak are valued for their heartwood. With other trees, such as maple and ash, the creamy sapwood is considered preferable. As a furniture maker, you have the choice of playing with color contrasts by mixing sapwood and heartwood together in the same piece or of keeping the tone of your work more consistent.

the skeletal backbone of the tree. At the center of the tree is the pith.

Trees in many climates grow more rapidly in spring than in summer. Within a single growth ring, this transition is revealed as changes in density and color. The interior of each annual ring, called the "earlywood," forms in the burst of spring growth and has cells of larger di-

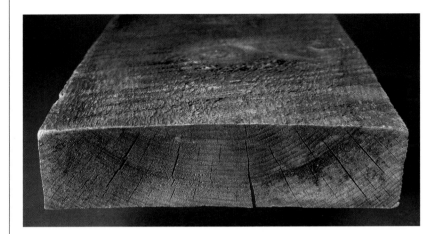

Wood shrinks as it dries. The ends of a board shrink before the interior, resulting in end checks. (Photo by Randy O'Rourke)

ameter and different color than the "late-wood" of summer growth.

Water and wood

Because the walls of wood cells are made of sponge-like material, they readily absorb moisture. Even a piece of "dry" wood, like the top of a dining table, gains and loses moisture as the humidity in the room changes with the weather and the season. Cell walls swell and shrink with variations in moisture content, changing in thickness but staying virtually constant in length. This is why, as humidity increases, a tabletop expands across the grain but remains constant in length.

The fact that wood fluctuates in dimension has required woodworkers throughout the centuries to come up with specialized techniques for permanently attaching one piece to another. These techniques are known collectively as "joinery" and are described in the next chapter.

DRYING WOOD A live tree felled for lumber contains two types of moisture: free water and bound water. Free water is that which has been flowing through the hollow cells;

bound water is that which has been absorbed in their cellulose walls. In a live tree, the combined weight of free and bound water can exceed the weight of the wood itself. Lumber that has been kiln-dried for furniture making contains no free water, and bound water constitutes only 6% to 8% by weight.

Removing all of the free water and most of the bound moisture isn't as simple as leaving a log out to dry, because wood shrinks as it dries, and uncontrolled shrinkage makes wood crack and split.

Imagine a freshly cut log lying on the ground. Moisture is evaporating through the bark and from the newly exposed ends. As the ring of wood around the log's circumference dries, it wants to shrink to a smaller diameter, but the interior hasn't lost much moisture yet and remains a constant size. As a result, the fibers of the shrinking exterior ring go into tension and break apart, causing radial checks (splits) that extend inward from the surface. As moisture evaporates from the ends of the log, the ends want to shrink but are held in place by their connection to the wetter interior wood. What happens? The ends of the log split to relieve the tension.

A freshly cut log left to dry on its own is likely to yield lumber degraded by cracks. The solution is to cut green logs into planks and seal the plank ends with paint or wax. The planks should be "stickered"—stacked flat with spacers in between to allow air to circulate freely—and kept away from the sun or an extremely dry environment. This procedure is called "air-drying," and the rule of thumb is that it takes up to one year per inch of board thickness.

Commercial lumber companies can't afford to keep wood in inventory long enough for it to air-dry, so they use kilns to remove the moisture. Boards are stacked in the kiln with spacers in between. Warm, moist air is circulated through the kiln. The humidity of the air is reduced gradually to keep it just a step ahead of the drying wood. This controlled, gradual process, called "kiln-drying," prevents checking and splitting if done correctly.

Long grain and end grain

To understand the meaning of long grain and end grain, again picture a board as a bunch of straws held together with glue. At the four sides of the board, we are looking at the outside of the straws—this is called "long grain" or "edge grain." At either end of the board, we are looking at the open ends of the straws, the "end grain."

WOOD TIP

Because end grain is open, it gains and loses moisture much more rapidly than long grain. Unless the ends of a drying board are sealed, they shrink faster than the rest of the board. Lumber that is going to be stored for any length of time should first have the ends sealed with wax, paint, or finish to prevent end checks. ■

The difference between long grain and end grain becomes significant when we glue wood together. The process of gluing two boards edge to edge can be looked at as reassembling the straws in wood with man-made adhesive instead of lignin. Because modern glues are actually stronger

CUTTING WITH THE GRAIN

Everyone has heard the expression "going against the grain." Its origin lies in the fact that the long cells that make up wood split apart from one another more easily than they break across their length. If you've ever split logs with an ax, you have probably noticed that the split follows the internal meanderings of the fibers rather than cutting straight down.

The blade of a handplane, chisel, or thickness planer can be thought of as a splitting ax. Once it enters the wood, its wedging action encourages wood to split along the grain. If you are cutting with the grain, the wood splits back up toward the surface and no harm results. But if you are cutting against the grain, the wood wants to split down toward the core and "tearout" occurs.

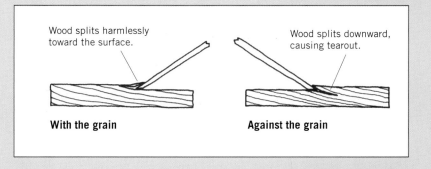

Wood splits harmlessly toward the surface.

Wood splits downward, causing tearout.

With the grain

Against the grain

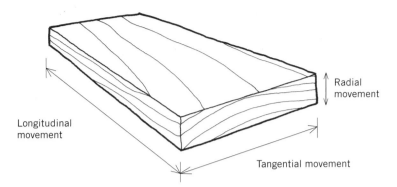

Longitudinal movement

Radial movement

Tangential movement

Wood expands as humidity increases and contracts as humidity decreases, but not equally in all directions. Tangential movement (more or less parallel to the growth rings) is greater than radial movement (perpendicular to the growth rings). Longitudinal movement (along the grain) is negligible.

than lignin, long-grain joints are very reliable. End-grain glue joints, on the other hand, are unreliable. The porous cells suck glue away from the contact point, and little bonding occurs.

Radial and tangential movement

When wood shrinks or expands across the grain, it doesn't move at a uniform rate in all dimensions. Movement perpendicular to the growth rings (radial movement) is about half that of movement tangential to the growth rings in hardwood species such as cherry and maple. This is significant. A dowel will become oval as moisture content changes. A flatsawn board will cup, as explained below.

Cup, bow, and twist

Wood warps in three ways: cupping, bowing, and twisting. Cup is a curve across the width, bow is a curve along the length, and twist is a spiral along the length.

In addition to changes in humidity, wood memory and internal stress are the major causes of wood movement. An example of memory occurs in wood that has

been steambent into a curve. Even after the wood has been thoroughly dried, an increase in humidity will encourage the crushed fibers on the inside of the curve to regain their shape, much as a crumpled, dried-up sponge regains its flat, square shape when you drop it in dishwater. As the crushed fibers swell, they force the wood back toward its original straightness. Good bentwood furniture counters memory by structurally locking each curve in place.

Internal stress comes from the way a particular tree has grown or been dried. Sometimes, as you rip a board along its length on a table saw, the two free ends don't stay parallel to each other. They bend together to pinch the sawblade, or they spread apart. This movement can come from growth stress seeking a new equilibrium as material is removed from the board. It can also result from stress imparted by improper kiln-drying or uneven moisture content in the wood.

Twist occurs because many trees grow with a slight spiral motion. A board that has been milled flat tends to recover some twist as changes in equilibrium occur

CUPPING

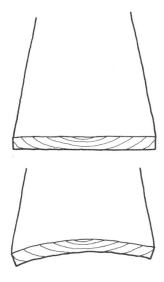

A flatsawn board cups away from the center of the tree as it dries.

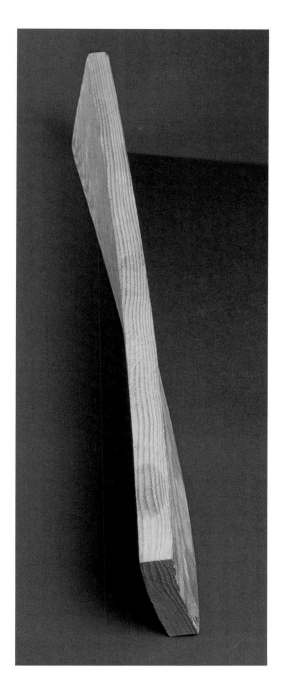

"Twist" is a spiral along a board's length, as shown in this Japanese fir. (Photo by Randy O'Rourke)

through wood removal or fluctuations in moisture content.

Removing wood from the surface of a board can cause it to cup, bow, or twist as the stress equilibrium is disturbed. Most of the time this is noticeable only if you are removing more than ⅛ in., but I once had the frustrating experience of trying to flatten an English brown oak tabletop that moved with every pass of my hand plane. Finally I had to shrug my shoulders and settle for something less than perfection. Such is the nature of woodworking.

If one side of a board is dampened, swelling will cause the board to cup away from that face. Conversely, a cup can be (temporarily) removed by wetting the inside or drying the outside.

Once a properly dried, hardwood board has been flattened and finished, bowing and twisting usually cease to be

major problems. But cupping is always a danger. As a flatsawn board dries, it cups in a curve opposite to its end-grain pattern (see the drawing above). As the board picks up moisture, it does the reverse. This is the result of differing radial and tangential shrinkage—the face of the board that was closer to the pith has more radial grain, whereas the far side has more tangential grain.

Types of Wood

There are many species of wood, but they divide into two broad groups—hardwoods and softwoods. As a general rule, hard-woods are deciduous (trees that shed their leaves annually) and softwoods are conif-erous (cone-bearing trees that stay green year-round).

Furniture makers generally prefer to work with hardwoods. They are stronger, warp less, come in a greater variety of grain patterns and colors, take a finish bet-ter, cut more cleanly, and leave less pitch residue on sawblades and planer knives. Softwoods, such as fir, pine, spruce, and redwood, are most often used in the con-struction trades for framing, trim, and fin-ish work in houses. A softwood such as southern yellow pine is actually denser and harder than a hardwood like basswood. But in general the hardwoods are harder and the softwoods softer.

Hardwoods come from all over the world and are distinguished from one an-other by density, color, porosity, and grain pattern. I generally work with domestic hardwoods such as cherry, maple, ash, oak, walnut, and poplar. Other furniture makers prefer the elegance or flamboyance of im-ports like bubinga, purpleheart, imbuye, rosewood, teak, mahogany, and ebony.

I choose domestic hardwoods because they are readily available, relatively afford-able, and often easier to work, and they offer a wide enough range of colors and grain patterns to suit my design needs. With imported woods one must consider whether or not they have been sustain-ably harvested and, if not, what the eco-logical cost of your wood habit may be. Also, breathing the sawdust from certain imported hardwoods, or skin contact with

FLATSAWN AND QUARTERSAWN PLANKS

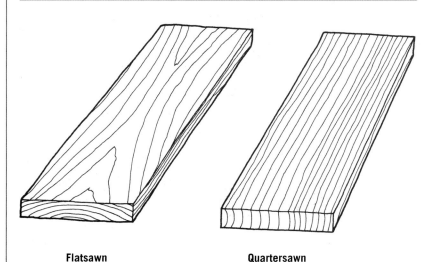

Flatsawn   **Quartersawn**

TWO METHODS OF SAWING A LOG FOR SOLID TIMBER

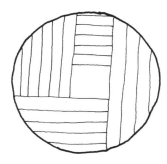

This method produces mostly flatsawn lumber.

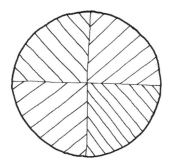

This method produces mostly quartersawn lumber.

them, is more likely to cause unpleasant, and even dangerous, allergic reactions.

Milling logs

When a log goes to the sawmill, the sawyer has a number of choices to make. If the log is going to be used as solid timber, it is milled to yield either flatsawn (also called plainsawn), quartersawn, or riftsawn planks. Flatsawn wood is identified by the arc pattern of its end grain and the flame pattern of its face grain. Quartersawn wood is identified by the parallel vertical strokes of its end grain and the straight parallel lines of its face grain. Riftsawn wood is similar to quartersawn, except that the end grain deviates more from the vertical.

Quartersawn and riftsawn boards are less likely to warp than flatsawn wood because they do not have the same sort of imbalance between radial and tangential grain on their two faces. However, riftsawn and quartersawn boards are also more costly to mill and create more waste than flatsawn lumber. For these reasons,

most of the wood found in lumberyards is flatsawn.

The drawing above shows two different approaches to milling a log, depending on whether flatsawn or quartersawn wood is desired. You might think that flatsawing would be better accomplished by starting at one side and cutting parallel planks all the way through, but generally the very center of a tree is unusable because of the pith and dense knots. When milling a furniture-grade log for flatsawn lumber, the

WOOD TIP

By the time wood gets from the sawmill to the typical lumberyard, boards from different trees within a species are intermixed. Because the color of wood varies from tree to tree, it becomes difficult to pick out matching wood for a large project. Some woodworkers solve this problem by having whole trees custom-milled at a local sawmill or with a portable chainsaw mill. ■

This selection of veneers shows the great range of color and grain pattern available in wood. (Photo by Randy O'Rourke)

sawyer cuts in from all four sides to avoid the center, as shown.

The sawyer must also decide how thick to cut the boards. If the wood is to be sold to a lumberyard, the sawyer probably wants to end up with boards at nominal sizes from 1 in. to 2 in. thick. A board that is going to be a specific thickness after drying must be milled oversize to allow for shrinkage in the kiln.

Veneer

A tremendous amount of lumber is cut for veneers, which are thin sheets of wood anywhere from approximately $\frac{1}{8}$ in. thick down to less than $\frac{1}{100}$ in. thick. Standard thickness for commercial veneer is $\frac{1}{36}$ in. to $\frac{1}{42}$ in., and getting thinner all the time. Veneers are used industrially to make plywood and other sheet goods. Furniture makers use veneers as surfaces on tables

CUTTING VENEERS

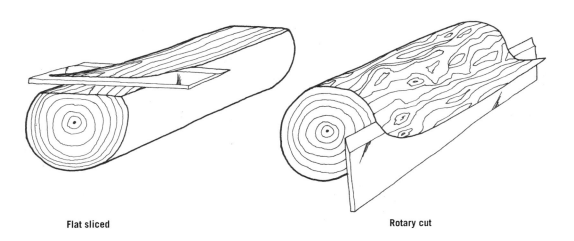

Flat sliced

Rotary cut

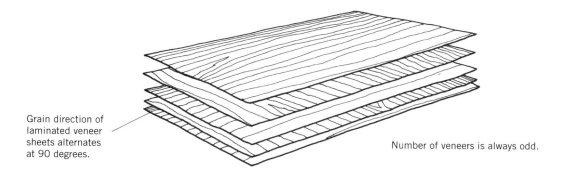

Grain direction of laminated veneer sheets alternates at 90 degrees.

Number of veneers is always odd.

and cabinets and for making curved forms through bent lamination.

Veneers can be either flat-sliced or rotary-cut (see the drawing on the facing page). Rotary-cut veneers have the wandering, loopy grain seen on construction plywood. Furniture makers prefer flat-sliced veneer, since it looks like either flat-sawn or quartersawn solid timber, depending on how it's cut. Flat-sliced veneers are restacked in the order they come off the tree and sold by the flitch. Working from a flitch, a furniture maker has the benefit of veneers whose grain and color match.

Plywood and particleboard

Much of the world's lumber harvest is used to make plywood and particleboard. Although the concept of plywood was introduced thousands of years ago, its manufacture only became practical with the development of high-quality adhesives during World War II. Plywood is made by laminating together sheets of veneer so the grain directions of adjacent pieces alternate at right angles (see the drawing above).

Always Odd

The thickness and number of veneers in plywood can vary. However, the number of veneers is always odd rather than even, so that the two exterior veneers will have parallel grain directions. This configuration cancels out any tendency of the plywood to cup due to changes in humidity—if one exterior sheet wants to expand and force the plywood to cup, the opposite sheet is expanding with an opposing, balancing force.

The long grain of each sheet prevents adjacent sheets from shrinking across their grain, and the entire assembly remains dimensionally stable. The other advantage of plywood is that, with grain running in two directions, it can't split the way solid wood does.

Although we will not be using plywood for the projects in this book, there are many furniture applications where plywood is a reasonable, and even desirable, solution. Cabinetmaking plywoods are distinguished from one another by the thickness, quality, and species of their interior veneers. Shop-grade birch plywood, which is commonly used for cabinet construction, has outside veneers of birch over thicker poplar substrates. It comes in thicknesses from ⅛ in. to ¾ in. and is a reliable, stable product.

Other plywoods of varying thicknesses come with fine hardwood exterior veneers over birch, poplar, luaun, or particleboard substrates. I sometimes buy ¼-in. hardwood-faced plywood to make drawer bottoms and cabinet backs. Thin (⅛-in.) plywood and flexible "bending plywood" are often used to create curved, laminated forms.

Man-made wood-based sheet materials are created by mixing wood chips and particles with glue. These materials go by names like particleboard, MDF (medium-density fiberboard), flakeboard, and hardboard, and are used similarly to plywood. The many varieties are differentiated by the size of the wood chips and the density with which they are compacted. I don't care for these composite sheet materials; they are heavy, because of the high percentage of glue, and weak, because there is no continuity of wood fiber. But they are used all the time to make forms, fixtures, and even fine, veneered furniture because of their inexpensiveness, stability, smoothness, and density.

Buying Wood

Hardwood suppliers are relatively hard to find and sometimes sell only to professional woodworkers. When I lived on the western slope of the Rocky Mountains, I had to drive 200 miles to Denver in order

Calculating Board Feet

Hardwood is priced and sold by a measurement called the "board foot," which is equal to 144 cu. in. (1 sq. ft. of a 1-in.-thick board). If all measurements are in inches, board footage is calculated by the formula: thickness x width x length ÷ 144.

For example, a 12/4 board that is 6 in. wide and 40 in. long contains 5 board feet (bd.ft.). If one of the measurements is in feet instead of inches, change the denominator to 12. For example, to determine the board footage of a plank of 8/4 cherry that is 9 in. wide and 10 ft. long, the calculation is as follows:

2 in. x 9 in. x 10 ft. ÷ 12 = 180 ÷ 12 = 15 bd. ft.

to purchase hardwoods. In more populated areas, you will probably be able to find a retail hardwood dealer nearby, or a wholesale yard that also sells retail. Conveniently, there are also a few companies that reliably sell wood by mail-order.

If you find a nearby supplier, the ideal arrangement is to be able to look through the stacks and pick out your own boards. Many yards don't allow selection, but if you can find one that does you'll be ahead of the game.

Your local building-supply company that deals in construction materials sells wood from bundles that have been cut to uniform thickness, width, and length. One 10-ft. fir 2x4 is much like another. Hardwoods are different. A "lift" of hardwood has been sorted for uniform thickness and grade, but the boards generally have random widths and lengths. No two boards in a bundle are exactly alike, and the quality within a single grade can vary dramatically.

Grading

Grading takes place at the sawmill, where boards are judged by width, proportion of sapwood on the better face, and the yield after cutting around knots. The best grade of hardwood in the traditional American grading system is FAS (Firsts and Seconds), followed by Select and Better, #1 Common, and #2 Common, which isn't good for much except making crates and pallets. In these days of global trade you may also run across FEQ (first European quality)

lumber, which is even better than FAS. I always buy the best grade available, which is usually FAS. But even FAS lumber doesn't always look good. I've picked through a thousand feet of FAS cherry to find only three excellent boards—the rest were bowed, too full of sapwood, or too knotty.

Hardwood is sold roughsawn or surfaced. Boards are called roughsawn because of the coarse surface left by the sawblade at the mill. The usual thicknesses available are 4/4 ("four-quarter," which is 1 in.), 5/4, 6/4, and 8/4 ("eight-quarter," which is 2 in.). Roughsawn hardwoods are required to measure at least their nominal thickness, so that a 4/4 roughsawn board measures at least a full inch. Surfaced boards, which have been run through a planer to smooth the faces, can lose up to $\frac{1}{4}$ in. of thickness in the process. A surfaced 4/4 board typically measures $\frac{13}{16}$ in. to $\frac{7}{8}$ in. thick.

Because boards surfaced at the lumberyard usually need to be remilled at home in order to be truly flat and straight, I prefer to buy roughsawn lumber, which leaves me with a thicker piece in the end. Some craftsmen take a block plane to the lumberyard in order to shave roughsawn boards for a glimpse of the grain. In any case, be sure to look wood over carefully before taking it home. End checks are to be expected, but a small surface check may be the only clue that a board has been improperly kiln-dried and is honeycombed with small cracks, which render it useless.

Joinery

JOINERY IS THE ART of attaching one piece of wood to another. Interlocking joints, mechanical fasteners, and adhesives, used singly or in combination, are the woodworker's joinery resources. Although screws and glue may serve a carpenter who is making a quick bookcase, fine furniture requires accurately cut interlocking joinery. The joint that holds a stretcher to a chair leg, or a drawer side to a drawer front, must be able to withstand the thousand stresses of daily use as well as cope with the seasonal movement of wood over generations.

Many modern joinery techniques were practiced thousands of years ago by the ancient Egyptians, then seem to have been forgotten in Europe until the late Middle Ages. After all these centuries, mortise and tenons and dovetails are still the preferred methods for joining wood. The only real advance in the joiner's art has been the mid-20th-century development of reliable glues.

A joint is considered to have mechanical strength to the extent that the pieces of wood physically interlock. It has glue strength to the extent that long grain to long grain contact permits a good glue bond. Sometimes mechanical strength or glue strength alone forms a sufficient joint; sometimes both are required.

The major factor the woodworker must cope with when joining wood together is wood movement. The other thing to keep in mind is that glue bonds well on long grain but poorly on end grain.

Coping with Wood Movement

Wood movement becomes a problem when two pieces of wood are joined together so the cross-grain expansion and contraction of one is inhibited by the long-grain stability of the other. A common breadboard provides a good example. As shown in the drawing below, the grain of the center board runs perpendicular to the grain of the cap pieces, and the boards meet in tongue-and-groove joints. One cap is pegged in place in the middle, while the other is pegged at the ends. No glue has been used.

Now, let's consider what will happen if the breadboard is introduced into a drier climate. The center board will want to shrink across its grain. The end with the single peg will have no problem. Shrinkage will take place toward the fixed point, and the only noticeable effect will be that the outside edges of the breadboard no longer line up.

The other end of the breadboard is a different story. Because the cap piece stays constant in length, the parts of the tongue that are pegged in place can't get any closer together. As a result, the center board is prevented from shrinking and will most likely split in the center to relieve the tension of pulling toward two fixed points. If the cap pieces had been spot-glued at the same locations, instead of pegged, the

same results would have occurred. If the caps had been glued along the entire length of the tongue and groove, stress would have occurred as with the two end pegs, and splits may have developed.

The stable way to peg breadboard ends is to make elongated peg holes in the tongue (actually in tenons protruding from the tongue) that allow it to move from side to side around the pegs, yet hold the cap snug against the shoulder.

Cabinet doors and tabletops present another challenge in coping with wood movement: Given wood's propensity for cupping and movement across the grain, how do you keep a wide expanse of wood flat and stable?

One traditional solution is board-and-batten construction. Several boards are placed edge to edge with two or three battens attached crossways to keep them flat (see the top left drawing on p. 18). If the boards haven't been glued to one another,

---

PROBLEMS OF WOOD MOVEMENT

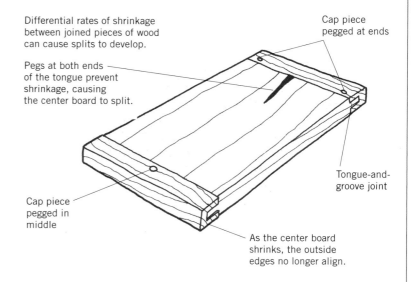

Differential rates of shrinkage between joined pieces of wood can cause splits to develop.

Pegs at both ends of the tongue prevent shrinkage, causing the center board to split.

Cap piece pegged at ends

Cap piece pegged in middle

Tongue-and-groove joint

As the center board shrinks, the outside edges no longer align.

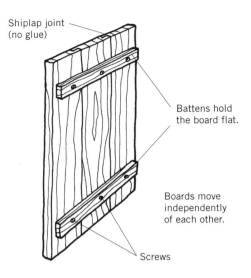

BOARD-AND-BATTEN CONSTRUCTION

Shiplap joint
(no glue)

Battens hold
the board flat.

Boards move
independently
of each other.

Screws

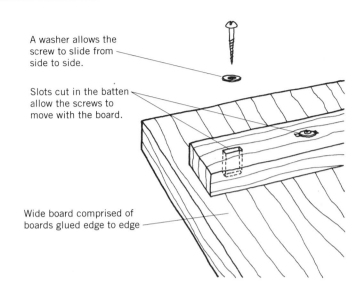

ALLOWING FOR WOOD MOVEMENT

A washer allows the
screw to slide from
side to side.

Slots cut in the batten
allow the screws to
move with the board.

Wide board comprised of
boards glued edge to edge

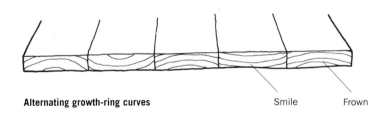

END-GRAIN ORIENTATION

All growth-ring curves the same

Alternating growth-ring curves

Smile   Frown

they can be screwed to the battens and left to shrink and expand independently of each other. The battens will hold them reasonably flat, and lapping the edges of the boards over one another will prevent see-through gaps between them.

When the boards are glued together to form one wide board, however, you have to allow for expansion and contraction across the entire width. This is commonly done by cutting slots in the battens to allow the screw shanks to move with the board. One way of doing so is shown in the drawing at top right.

Two strategies for assembling a tabletop are shown in the drawing at bottom left. The end-grain orientation of each board affects the movement of the entire panel. When the end grain of every board curves the same way, the panel tends to react to humidity as if it were a single board. Therefore, affixing a batten with a single screw in the center will prevent the panel from cupping when humidity decreases and the center wants to lift. Two other screws, one slotted near each end, will prevent the edges from lifting when humidity increases.

The second strategy to minimize cupping is to alternate growth-ring curves: smile, frown, smile, frown, and so on. Although the boards may cup, they will tend to cancel each other out so the overall surface stays fairly flat. A third strategy is to place the best-looking side of each board up (my usual method) and let the growth rings fall where they may.

The most sophisticated method for making wide, flat wood surfaces in solid timber is frame-and-panel construction (see the drawing at right). The vertical components of the frame are called "stiles" and the horizontal components are "rails." Because the length of the grain runs around the perimeter of the frame, the only dimensional change in response to humidity takes place across the width of the stiles, which are generally kept fairly narrow. The panel floats in a groove, without glue, so it is free to shrink and expand but cannot cup.

FRAME-AND-PANEL CONSTRUCTION

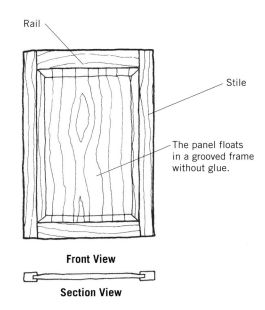

Rail

Stile

The panel floats in a grooved frame without glue.

Front View

Section View

TYPES OF JOINTS

There are four basic applications for joinery in furniture making (see the drawing below). The first is where pieces of wood meet long grain to long grain, as in a tabletop or assembling thin boards to make a thicker one. The second is where the end of one board runs into the edge of another, as in a door frame or table

BASIC JOINERY APPLICATIONS

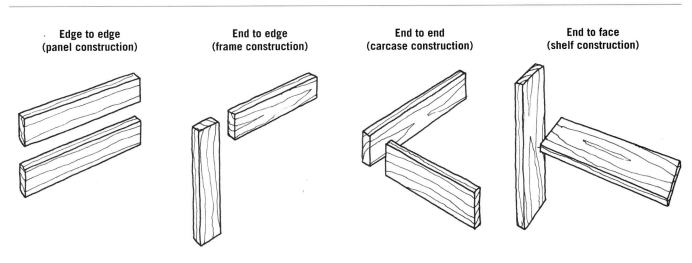

Edge to edge
(panel construction)

End to edge
(frame construction)

End to end
(carcase construction)

End to face
(shelf construction)

THE "ALAN PETERS" SHELF JOINT

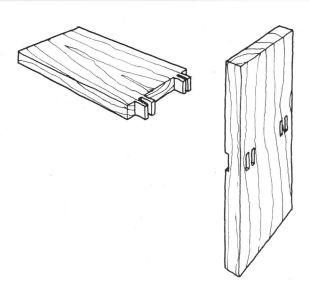

WOOD TIP

You may not always choose the strongest joint. Sometimes the look you desire, the time available, or the tools at hand make a lesser joint preferable. For example, although dovetails are stronger and more durable, box joints are perfectly adequate for case piece assembly and more economical to make in production. ■

apron. The third is where two pieces of wood meet end to end to form a corner, as in case-piece construction (boxes, chests, and drawers). The fourth is where the end grain of one meets the face of another, as a shelf does.

In the first instance, no mechanical joint is needed if the boards meet cleanly. Glue creates a bond between the parallel wood fibers that is stronger than the natural bond provided by lignin, so the joint becomes the strongest part of the whole. Some woodworkers insert dowels, splines, or biscuits in an edge joint, but these serve mainly to align the boards while gluing.

The second instance is typified by the joint between a rail and a stile. The main methods of assembling this joint are mortise and tenon, biscuit, dowel, and tongue and groove. The mortise and tenon is the best joint in this category because it provides extensive mechanical and glue strength.

In case-piece construction, the top-of-the-line corner joint is the dovetail. A second-best alternative is the box joint, followed by spline and tongue-and-groove joints, dowels, screws, and nails.

For a shelf, there are two best joints. One is the sliding dovetail, which is difficult to cut accurately and assemble across wide surfaces. The other, my favorite, is the "Alan Peters joint," which I have named in recognition of the English furniture maker from whom I learned it (see the drawing above). Lesser alternatives for attaching shelves to cases are dowel, biscuit, tongue and groove, and dado joints.

An illustrated glossary of basic wood joints follows. Projects 2 and 3 provide detailed instructions for cutting the two most important joints: the mortise and tenon (see pp. 93–105) and the dovetail (see pp. 106–115).

Mortise-and-tenon joints

A mortise is a hole, usually rectangular, cut in a piece of wood. A tenon is a tongue, projecting from another piece of wood, made to fit in the mortise. Variations on the mortise and tenon include blind and through tenons, the bridle joint, and the haunched tenon. The blind tenon is invisible after the joint is assembled because the mortise is cut in the wood from only one side. The through tenon remains visible after assembly, since the mortise is cut completely through. A bridle joint is essentially an open mortise and tenon. The mortise is open on three sides, and the tenon is exposed on two sides after assembly.

A haunch adds strength to the mortise-and-tenon joint by creating extra mechanical interlock and long-grain glue surface (see the top left drawing on p. 22). Often, haunches are employed for the more practical purpose of filling a groove that has been ploughed through a door stile to hold a panel. Otherwise, the groove would show as a square hole in the edge of the door.

The mechanical strength of a properly proportioned mortise and tenon is considerable. If the tenon is glued, pinned, or wedged in place, the joint will not pull, twist, or rock apart. A well-proportioned mortise and tenon also offers extensive glue strength—the long-grain cheeks of the tenon meet the long-grain cheeks of the mortise at right angles to one another. At

MORTISE AND TENON

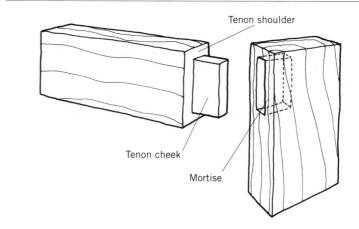

Tenon shoulder

Tenon cheek

Mortise

TENON VARIATIONS

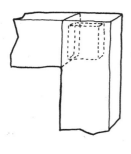

Blind tenon

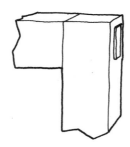

Through tenon

Bridle joint

SOPHISTICATED VERSIONS OF THE MORTISE AND TENON

Haunched tenon with grooved stile

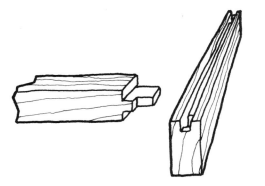

Multiple mortise and tenon

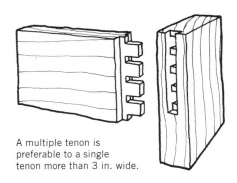

A multiple tenon is preferable to a single tenon more than 3 in. wide.

A BETTER SOLUTION FOR A WIDE TENON

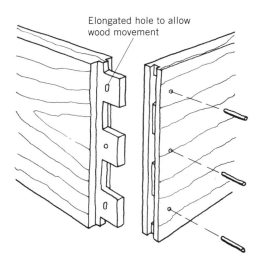

Elongated hole to allow wood movement

first glance, we might expect the differential movement between the cheeks of a tenon and the cheeks of a mortise to compromise the joint over time. In practice, unless a tenon is particularly wide, there is no problem. In a well-cut mortise and tenon, only a portion of the glue surface has to stay bonded in order to maintain the in-

tegrity of the joint; most stress is handled by the joint's mechanical properties.

The rule for proportion is that the length of a tenon should be at least twice, and preferably three times, its thickness. In frames, tenon thickness is often determined by the rule that the shoulder on either side of a mortise should be as thick as the mortise itself. Shoulders that are too thin are liable to break out under stress.

The width of a tenon can vary quite a bit, depending on the width of the rail from which it protrudes. However, if a tenon gets too wide (say, over 3½ in.), differential shrinkage between the cheeks of the tenon and the cheeks of the mortise can cause glue failure or splitting in the joint. A traditional solution to the problem of wide tenons (and one that doesn't work so well) is to substitute a series of smaller haunched tenons, as shown in the drawing at right above, to spread the stress of shrinkage more evenly. A better solution would be to

INSERTED TENONS

An inserted tenon has matching mortises cut in both sides of the joint and a separate piece of wood (a "loose tenon") milled to fit tightly between them. In strength and function, an inserted tenon is equivalent to a standard mortise-and-tenon joint. Inserted tenons are often used in production shops.

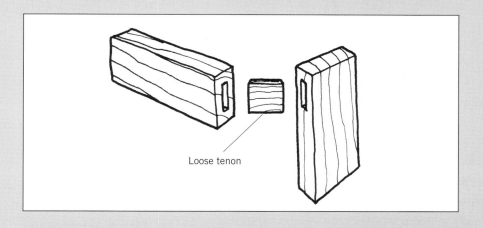

Loose tenon

peg the tenons in extra-wide mortises through oval slots to allow for sideways movement (see the bottom left drawing on the facing page).

A related joint is the round mortise and tenon, which is, in effect, like a dowel joint, and suffers the defects of that joint, as described below.

Dowel joints

The dowel joint is probably the most common method of joinery used by woodworkers and manufacturers, but popularity should not be confused with quality. The dowel joint has inherent defects that limit its effectiveness. In fact, if you've seen manufactured chairs and tables with the

DOWEL JOINT

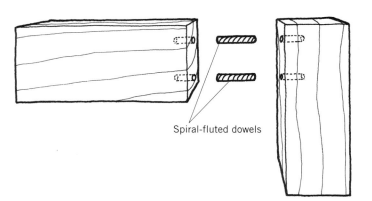

Spiral-fluted dowels

DOWEL HOLE

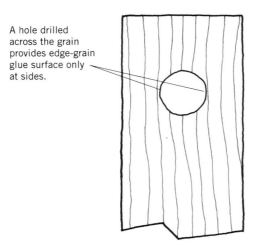

A hole drilled across the grain provides edge-grain glue surface only at sides.

legs falling off, you've probably noticed that they are joined with dowels.

Dowel joints are popular because they are easy to make. Matching holes are drilled in two pieces of wood and dowel pins are glued between them. Unfortunately, a hole drilled across the grain provides very little long-grain glue surface (see the

drawing at left). To make matters worse, dowels lose their round shape over time because of differing radial and tangential shrinkage; they become oval pegs in round holes.

In spite of their limitations, dowels are a good choice in some situations, including:

- joining together a prototype that does not have to last

- joining parts of a continuous chair arm, where end grain butts against end grain

- aligning boards while gluing a tabletop together

As with a mortise and tenon, the depth of a dowel hole should be at least twice, and preferably three times, its diameter. Dowels of various diameters can be purchased at lumberyards and hardware stores in the form of long rods or precut pins. Of the two, precut pins have been milled to more accurate diameters and have spiral or straight grooves cut along their lengths as glue channels. The chan-

DOVETAIL JOINTS

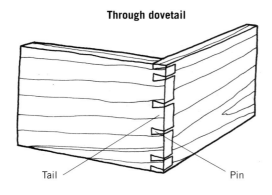

Through dovetail

Tail

Pin

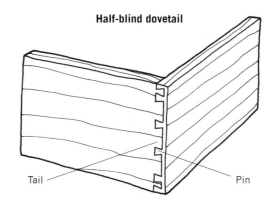

Half-blind dovetail

Tail

Pin

nels allow glue to escape from the hole as the dowel is driven in; otherwise, hydraulic pressure could split the wood.

Dovetails

Dovetails are the classic joint for solid-wood case-piece construction. They create strong mechanical interlock and plenty of long-grain contact for glue. Because dovetails are used only where the ends of two boards meet, wood movement is never a problem—the boards move in unison.

There are three basic dovetail variations: through, half-blind, and hidden-miter. The choice of which to use is generally an aesthetic one. I have never had occasion to cut hidden-miter dovetails, which are more difficult to make and don't show after the joint is assembled.

Box joints

The box joint, or finger joint, is used for the same applications as dovetails. It is a strong joint, with plenty of long-grain glue

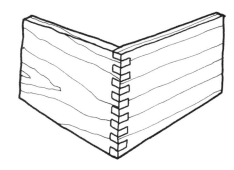

contact, but seems to be rarely used in fine furniture. Perhaps this is because the box joint is best suited to machine production and conveys little of the sense of hand-made quality that a dovetail imparts.

Tongue-and-groove joints

The tongue-and-groove joint has many applications, as in flooring, siding, and other situations where boards meet edge to edge.

TONGUE-AND-GROOVE JOINTS

Tongue-and-groove edge joint

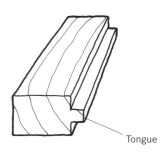

Tongue

Groove

Tongue-and-groove carcase joint

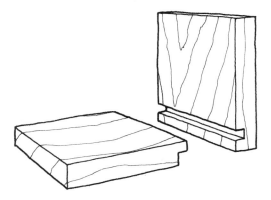

SPLINED EDGE JOINT

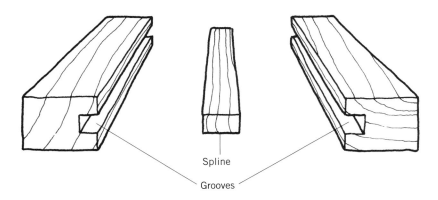

Spline

Grooves

Though it can be considered a form of overkill, tongue and groove is occasionally used in place of a simple edge joint for tabletops, because it provides extra glue surface within the joint, a mechanical bond, and a surefire means of lining boards up during assembly.

Tongue-and-groove joinery is also used for case-piece construction. It doesn't form a first-rate corner joint in solid wood because the intersections are all end grain to long grain, resulting in weak glue bonds.

However, tongue and groove is a great joint for plywood cases, where layers of long grain are exposed in every surface of the joint.

In commercial cabinets and doors, rails are often attached to stiles with a tongue-and-groove joint. This is greatly inferior to a mortise and tenon, with relatively little mechanical and glue strength.

Spline joints

Spline joints are similar to tongue-and-groove joints, except that the tongue

SPLINED MITER JOINTS

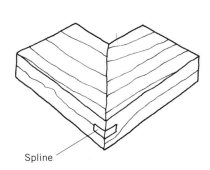

Spline

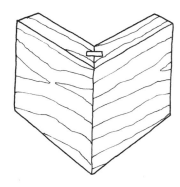

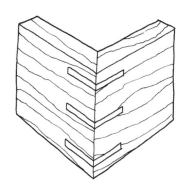

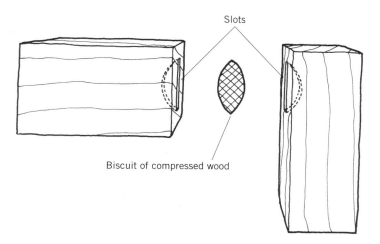

Slots

Biscuit of compressed wood

(spline) is a separate piece of wood that fits into grooves cut in both sides of the joint. Spline joints are useful in most of the same situations as tongue-and-groove joints. Additionally, they are used to provide mechanical strength, glue surface, and registration for mitered corners. The grain direction of a spline is crucial. It should be oriented to shrink and expand in harmony with the grain of the grooves. For a splined edge joint, the grain should run along the spline's length. For a splined miter joint, the grain should run across the spline.

Biscuit joinery

Biscuit (or plate) joinery is a more recent technology that works like an inserted tenon and combines aspects of spline and dowel joinery. Biscuits can be an efficient substitute for splines, dowels, and tenons in applications as varied as edge-gluing boards, joining mitered corners, and assembling frames.

A biscuit joiner has a small circular sawblade that is used to cut matching slots in two pieces of wood. The biscuit inserted between them is a thin, fish-shaped piece of compressed wood. As moisture is absorbed during glue-up, biscuits expand tightly into their slots.

For some applications, such as kitchen cabinet door frames, biscuits can be a reliable and cost-efficient substitute for mortise-and-tenon joinery. However, I am skeptical of their durability in joints that work a lot, such as table aprons or, especially, chair rails. There just isn't enough meat in the joint to cope with long-term stress.

Sliding dovetails

The sliding dovetail can be used to attach battens to boards, drawer sides to over-hanging faces, and dividers to the insides of cabinets, among other things. Mechanically, it is a very strong joint. Glue

SCREWS AND NAILS

A friend who repairs antique furniture first explained to me the incompatibility of screws with wood. Over and over, he finds old furniture that has fallen apart because the screws have worked loose. Wood surrounding a screw hole gradually compresses and wears away as it rubs against the metal of the screw with each season's expansion and contraction.

In furniture built to last, the few legitimate uses for screws include attaching a door or tabletop to battens, mounting hinges and hardware, or perhaps putting a plywood back on a solid-wood cabinet.

With all that said, screws are an indispensable part of the furniture workshop. They are invaluable for assembling mock-ups, jigs, and fixtures. I keep a supply of drywall screws on hand for just these uses—they rarely break, and the Phillips-head slot makes them easy to drive with an electric drill.

Nails are more suited to carpentry than to fine furniture making. They provide a dubious long-term mechanical bond, and the movement of wood over time will gradually back a nail out of its hole. The main use for nails in my shop is to make jigs and fixtures.

SLIDING DOVETAIL

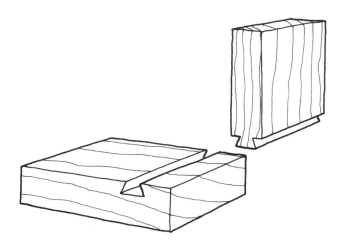

strength varies, depending on the grain orientation between the boards. If the grain of the dovetail runs crosswise to that of the host piece, the joint should be glued in only one spot to allow for shrinkage and expansion.

Cutting a successful sliding dovetail requires exactitude. The difference between a joint that won't slide together and a joint with loose shoulders is only a few thousandths of an inch. And the wider the wood, the more difficult it gets, because any amount of cupping affects the cutting and assembly considerably.

Introduction to
Woodworking Machines

MACHINERY HAS BECOME such an accepted part of the modern workshop that the meaning of the phrase "handmade furniture" has changed. Once used to describe furniture constructed entirely with hand tools, "handmade" now signifies furniture built by an individual craftsman rather than a factory, even if that individual works entirely with power tools. No one complains that the modern craftsman mills rough boards to thickness with electrically powered table saws, jointers, and planers instead of a ripsaw and handplanes. Machines are simply more efficient for milling lumber.

It would be wrong, however, to draw the conclusion that machines and power tools are an across-the-board replacement for hand tools. In fact, quite the opposite is true. There is little a machine can do that a craftsman skilled in the use of hand tools can't do, but there are many situations where the work of hand tools cannot reasonably be attempted with machinery.

An excellent approach to acquiring woodworking craftsmanship is to begin by mastering the use of hand skills for cutting joinery, handplanes for flattening and smoothing wood, and machinery for basic milling operations. Later, with confidence in your hand skills, you may choose to substitute machine work for handwork in situations where it will save time without compromising quality.

THE ESSENTIAL TOOLS

The basic stationary machines for furniture making are the table saw, bandsaw, jointer, thickness planer, drill press, grinder, and lathe. The most commonly used hand-held power tools are the router, drill, biscuit joiner, circular saw, and various sanders.

Although this book emphasizes hand skills and explains how to work lumber without power tools, it generally assumes that the reader has access to basic woodworking machines for the process of milling rough lumber to finished thickness, width, and length. If you don't have your own machinery, you can often obtain access to it through the continuing education

SAFETY TOP 10

CONSCIOUSNESS OF SAFETY is the first requirement of good craftsmanship. Ten important shop safety procedures are listed below. Safety tips specific to each woodworking machine are discussed in the relevant sections.

1 **Wear hearing and eye protection** when using saws, routers, sanders, and other equipment. I know woodworkers who are kept awake at night by the sound of imaginary routers because they worked without headphones or earplugs for too many years. To keep dust and splinters out of my eyes, I rely on the plastic lenses of my prescription glasses, but they are barely adequate. I strongly recommend wearing safety glasses, goggles, or a face shield when using power equipment.

2 **Keep your workshop clean and neat** so you won't trip over a scrap of wood or an extension cord at an inopportune moment.

3 **Tie up long hair and don't wear loose clothing or jewelry.** I met a woman whose hair had caught in a planer during a college woodworking course. Fortunately for her, the instructor instantly disengaged the clutch; otherwise her scalp would have been ripped off.

4 **Don't use machinery when you're tired or when you have consumed alcohol or motor-skill-impairing drugs.** Woodworking equipment is dangerous enough when you are fully alert, so why increase the odds against you? My personal rule is not to use machinery after 9 p.m., when I assume I'll be more tired.

5 **Focus on what you are doing at all times,** and take a break if your mind starts to wander. You are most likely to have accidents when performing repetitive operations.

6 **If you're not comfortable** making a particular cut or aren't sure it's safe, get advice or help before you try it. Find a friendly professional woodworker to ask.

7 **Keep sawblades sharp.** The harder you have to push, the less control you have.

8 **Be prepared for accidents.** Consider these questions: Where are your telephone, your first-aid kit, and the nearest person who can help? Can you give clear directions to your shop over the telephone? Are you familiar with basic first-aid and tourniquet procedures?

9 **If a serious injury occurs, call 911** for an ambulance rather than have a friend drive you to the hospital. What would your friend do if you went into shock on the highway?

10 **If you should be so unfortunate** as to sever any fingers, wrap them in wet gauze and take them with you to the hospital in case they can be reattached.

program at your local community college. You might also look for shared workshop space nearby.

This chapter presents the basic woodworking machines and power tools, explaining what they do and how to use them safely. More detailed, step-by-step instructions on using the table saw, jointer, and thickness planer are offered in the chapter "Milling a Board Four-Square" on pp. 77–92. If you already have your own machinery and feel comfortable using it, you might look at this chapter as a review. If you are just learning to use machinery, a prudent addition to reading this material would be to find some hands-on instruction.

SHOP SAFETY

Any discussion of woodworking machinery should begin with shop safety. Woodworking machines are made to cut, slice, chop, abrade, drill, and shave materials that are considerably more resistant than human flesh. Machines are dangerous when used carelessly and wonderfully helpful when used well.

Wherever woodworkers gather, stories of accidents and near-misses come up sooner or later. A Danish furniture maker in Philadelphia told me of coming to work one morning and finding fingers strewn about the table saw. Apparently, at the end of the previous day, his partner's German shepherd had jumped against the man's back just as he was making a cut, jolting the man's hand through the blade.

I've seen a couple of bad accidents myself, and both were the result of carelessness by the injured person. Perhaps our terminology is wrong. "Accident" implies that the injured person is a victim of circumstances beyond his or her control; in most cases it may be more appropriate to say that the injured party suffers the consequences of his or her own carelessness.

Health concerns

Breathing sawdust isn't healthy; it can be allergenic, toxic, and carcinogenic. The sawdust from some imported woods, including teak, is particularly harmful and is known to cause skin rashes and respiratory problems. Several studies have shown that woodworkers have a high rate of nasal cancer.

An efficient mask is minimum safety equipment where dust is concerned, whether you're running a table saw or sweeping the floor. However, the best way to deal with sawdust is to install a good dust-collection system—one that is convenient to use even when you're in a rush. Now that we have one at the Center for Furniture Craftsmanship, I would never willingly work wood without it. Even a little sawdust has always affected my sinuses and aggravated my allergies.

Masks range from thin paper models to thick rubber ones with replaceable cartridge filters. Heavy-duty masks are generally unpleasant to wear, so some compromise needs to be made between efficiency and comfort. The mask I currently prefer has a light, metal body with replaceable filter pads.

Some of the solvents and finishes used
in furniture finishing are also allergenic,
toxic, and carcinogenic. Petroleum distil-
lates in commercial oil finishes, naphtha,
and benzene are all suspect. Over many
years of use I became allergic to turpen-
tine, with which I thinned oil finishes on
the theory that it was a "natural" product
and therefore safe. Now I use mineral spirits, which at least don't make me sneeze.

THE TABLE SAW

The table saw is the first piece of major
equipment most woodworkers purchase.
This versatile tool can be used to make
straight cuts along the length of a board
(ripping), across the width (crosscutting),
or at any angle up to 45° (mitering). The
table saw can also be used to cut grooves
and various types of joints, such as the
box joint, tenon, bridle joint, and tongue
and groove.

A table saw should be sturdily built
with a strong motor. An underpowered,
undersized saw won't handle hardwoods
satisfactorily. Variables to consider in purchasing a saw include blade diameter, volt-
age, and horsepower.

Table saws are sized according to the
diameter of the blade they take. Common
sizes are 8 in., 10 in., and 12 in., though
larger and smaller ones exist. The stan-

TABLE-SAW ANATOMY

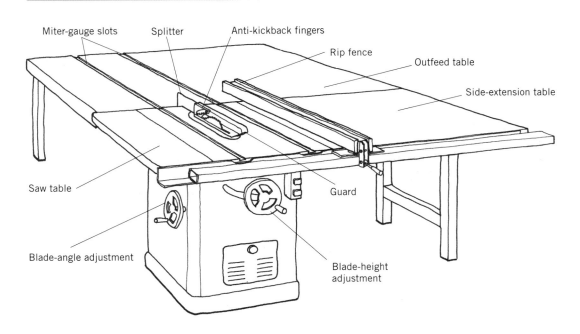

Miter-gauge slots   Splitter   Anti-kickback fingers

Rip fence

Outfeed table

Side-extension table

Saw table

Guard

Blade-angle adjustment

Blade-height
adjustment

A rip fence is used when sawing a board along its length.

TOOL TIP

Before using a new table saw, check to be sure that the table is mounted in line with the blade. This can be done by putting a long straightedge against the side of the fully raised blade and measuring to see that it is parallel with the miter-gauge slots that run through the table. If the blade and the table are out of alignment, the saw is unsafe and the table must be loosened where it joins the cabinet and be repositioned. ■

dard among furniture makers is a 10-in. cabinet saw. Fully raised at 90°, a 10-in. blade will cut through about 3 in. of wood.

A 10-in. saw should have a motor of at least 2½ hp, wired for 220-volt single-phase or for three-phase electricity. Normal 120-volt house current doesn't have enough kick to power a sawblade through a 2-in. oak board.

Table-saw accessories

A basic table saw can be greatly improved by adding auxiliary tables and a good rip fence. An extension table to the side and an outfeed table behind the saw make it easier and safer to cut large sheets of plywood and long boards, especially if you work alone. You can buy ready-made extension tables for some saws, but they are also easy to build yourself. The width of the side-extension table is often determined by the capacity of the rip fence. In our shop the extension table is wide enough to accommodate a 53-in.-capacity rip fence, and the outfeed table extends 42 in. beyond the saw table.

TOOL TIP

It's important that you take time to align the rip fence parallel with the blade. If the fence angles in toward the blade, the space between them narrows as wood travels through, which can cause binding. If the fence angles outward at all, the wood tends to pull away from it as the cut proceeds. This is because the wood wants to track straight ahead in line with the saw kerf. In either case, the risk of kickback increases unacceptably. ■

A rip fence is used when sawing a board along its length. The rip fence should be sturdy, adjust and remove easily, and have faces that are truly perpendicular to the table. I particularly like the fence system made by Biesemeyer.

Crosscutting is done with the aid of a miter gauge or sliding table. Crosscutting

Attach a wooden fence to the face of the miter gauge for increased utility.

A miter gauge comes as standard equipment with most table saws. It slides in table slots on either side of the blade and can be set to cut any angle up to 45°. Lengthening the face of the gauge by attaching a straight piece of wood increases accuracy, control, and versatility. Another trick is to line the face of the guide with PSA (pressure-sensitive-adhesive) sandpaper to keep wood from sliding.

The best accessory for accurate and safe crosscutting is a sliding table. Unlike the miter gauge, which runs in one slot and can wobble a bit, a well-made sliding table rides securely in both miter-gauge slots and is designed to handle longer and wider stock. Sliding tables are available commercially or can be made in your own workshop. When you are using a sliding table, it is important to keep your hands away from the slot where the blade exits the back of the fence as you push through. At the Center for Furniture Craftsmanship, we've limited the forward travel of our sliding table

freehand against the rip fence may be the most common and dangerous mistake that beginners make. Never do it! If you crosscut a board with one end against the rip fence and a corner pulls just a hair off the fence, the other end of the board jams into the blade and flies back at you. The hand holding the board may be drawn into the blade before you can react.

A sliding table or a miter gauge should always be used when crosscutting on the table saw.

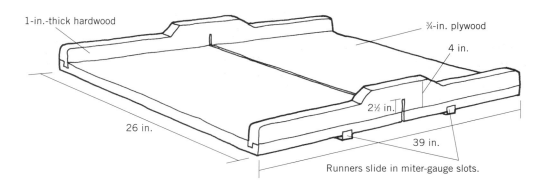

1-in.-thick hardwood

¾-in. plywood

4 in.

2½ in.

26 in.

39 in.

Runners slide in miter-gauge slots.

by screwing wooden stops into the miter-gauge slots of the extension table.

Sawblades

Sawblades available for table saws include rip, crosscut, combination, dado, laminate, and plywood blades. They vary from one another according to the shape, set, number, and spacing of the teeth. There are also choices to be made between carbide and steel teeth, and between standard and thin-kerf blades. In general, carbide is better than steel because it stays sharp much longer. The only situation in which I prefer steel is when cutting wood that may contain nails or screws. Better to ruin a cheap blade than a good one. Thin-kerf blades, which leave a kerf just under $\frac{3}{32}$ in. wide instead of ⅛ in. or wider, can be good for rip-

TOOL TIP

Keep sawblades sharp. Over time, pitch from wood adheres to the sides of a blade and reduces cutting efficiency. To remove pitch, run a blade under hot water and rub with a rag or stiff brush. ■

TOOL TIP

Sawblades should be changed with the saw unplugged. The nut that holds the blade on the arbor does not need to be white-knuckle tight; because the arbor thread is reversed, the rotation of the blade has a self-tightening effect. ■

ping because they remove less wood and, consequently, don't have to work as hard.

I suggest starting with a good-quality, standard-thickness, carbide combination blade, even though it may seem costly. A good blade is balanced and set to give a cleaner, smoother cut; a bad blade is misery to work with. A combination blade is all you need to successfully rip, crosscut, and miter solid wood. Very occasionally I switch to a rip blade, but only when I have a whole lot of ripping to do at one time.

Dado blades are used to cut dadoes (flat-bottomed grooves cut through a board) and rabbets (grooves cut along an edge). The better type of dado blade has six or seven component blades that can be assembled to any thickness from ¼ in. to $\frac{13}{16}$ in. by sixteenths. The inferior kind,

SAFETY TIPS FOR THE TABLE SAW

1 Never let go of a piece of wood in the middle of a cut, lest it end up in your face or groin. Push wood through until it passes the blade entirely.

2 Always keep wood against the fence when ripping.

3 Make sure that your saw is equipped with the right safety equipment. A splitter is absolutely mandatory for safety.

4 Set blade height so the gullets between the teeth just clear the wood.

5 When crosscutting or mitering, always back the wood with a miter guide or sliding table. Never involve the rip fence.

6 Use a push stick for ripping.

7 Unplug the saw when changing blades.

8 Keep blades sharp.

commonly known as a "wobbler," is a single blade whose teeth adjust on a cam to any width from ¼ in. to ¾ in.

Safety equipment

More accidents seem to occur on the table saw than on any other woodworking machine. Accordingly, many different kinds of safety devices have been developed to keep your hands away from the sawblade and to prevent the saw from throwing wood back at you. Kickback, which can be strong enough to send a 2x4 through a wall 20 ft. away, is usually caused by wood binding between the blade and the fence, then lifting over the back of the blade and being flung at the operator. It can also result when the ends of a board pinch together as they pass the sawblade, or from careless operation of the saw. The two dangers of kickback are, first, that the returning board can hit you, and, second, that if you are holding the wood with a hand beyond the sawblade, your hand can be drawn into the blade before you have a chance to let go.

Safety equipment for the table saw includes hold-downs, anti-kickback fingers, splitters, blade guards, and push sticks. The integrated splitter, anti-kickback-fingers, and blade-guard unit that comes as standard equipment on a new table saw is often poorly engineered and aggravating to use. However, the splitter is pretty much the single most important piece of safety equipment you can have. It is a thin piece of metal rising just behind the sawblade that rides in the kerf and prevents wood from drifting away from the rip fence. It also keeps the ends of a board from pinching the blade as they retension themselves during a cut. We use an aftermarket, removable splitter made by Biesemeyer on one of our table saws (see top left photo on the facing page) and a shop-made splitter on the other.

The blade guard is generally a clear plastic cover that lifts as wood passes underneath. It does a good job of keeping your hands from the blade but also has certain disadvantages. The guard can make it difficult to watch the blade meet the wood; it gets in the way when ripping narrow strips; and it has to be removed entirely when a sliding table is in use. For

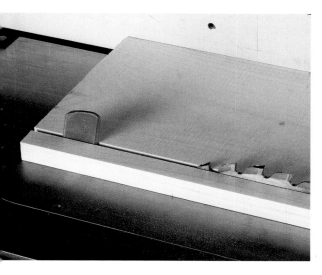

A splitter is one of the most important pieces of safety equipment in the shop.

A magnetic featherboard keeps wood from drifting off of the fence.

these reasons, we have installed an aftermarket blade guard (also made by Biesemeyer) that is easily removed.

Hold-downs are devices that exert pressure to keep wood against the saw table or the fence during a rip cut. A popular version, called a fingerboard or featherboard, is a piece of wood with parallel saw kerfs cut into one end to leave thin, flexible fingers. Another useful design is the magnetic featherboard. One circumstance in which featherboards are helpful is production milling where many boards of identical dimension are ripped at the same setting. Another is when ripping curved slats to width (see the photo at bottom right).

Push sticks keep your hands out of danger when ripping on a table saw (or when using a jointer). It is especially important to use them when ripping wood to widths less than 4 in. Push sticks can be cut in a variety of shapes and are usually made out of plywood, which won't split at an inopportune moment the way solid wood

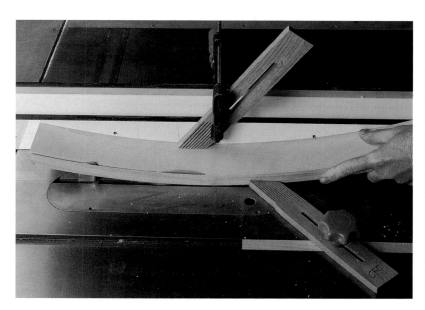

Using featherboards to hold down a curved slat allows you to rip the piece safely.

PUSH-STICK DESIGNS

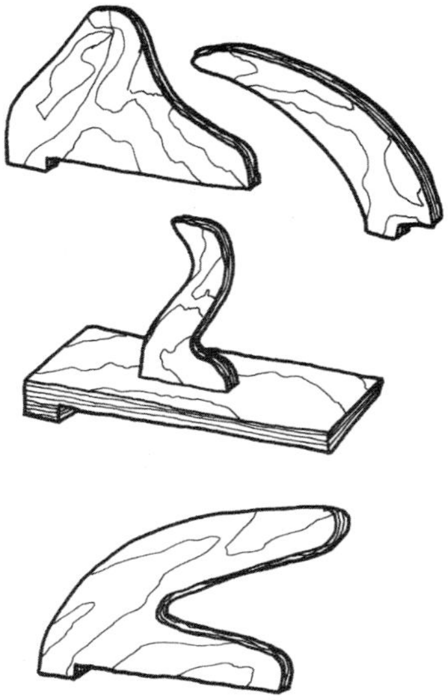

might. I prefer push-stick designs that extend forward over the wood, holding it down at the same time as they push it forward.

For certain types of cuts, safety equipment gets in the way and must be removed. As a general rule, though, it is best to use every reasonable safety precaution when possible.

The Bandsaw

If I could have only one piece of machinery in my workshop, it would be a bandsaw. This versatile tool can do anything from the brute work of resawing a hardwood beam into planks to the delicate work of cutting curves for a cabriole leg.

I often use the bandsaw in situations where others might use a table saw be-

BANDSAW ANATOMY

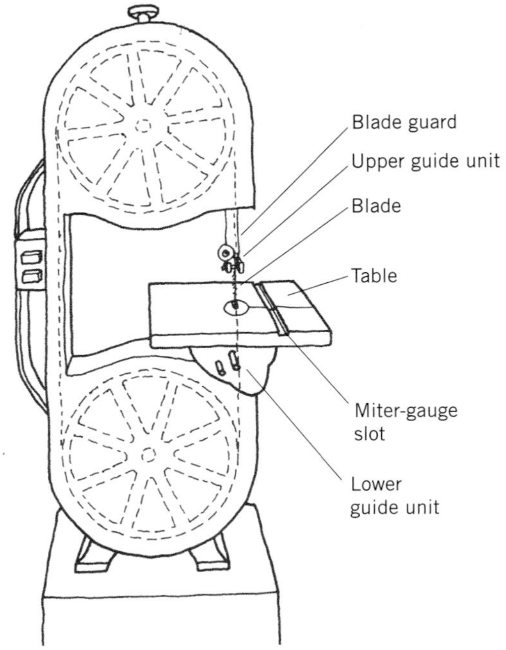

cause the bandsaw is friendlier and safer. A prime example is ripping rough lumber to approximate width at the start of the milling process (see p. 80). Bowed or cupped boards that might tend to jam or kick back on a table saw cut smoothly on the bandsaw. On the other hand, the table saw is definitely better suited to making straight, square finish cuts at the conclusion of the milling process.

A bandsaw consists of a continuous ribbon of sawblade held in tension between two (or sometimes three) wheels, one of which is driven by a motor. The blade runs through upper and lower guide units made up of blocks or bearings to either side and a bearing behind; the upper unit also has a blade guard attached. Bandsaw tables can tilt to make angled cuts up to and beyond 45°.

Bandsaws are specified according to the diameter of their wheels. The minimum size for amateur and small professional shops is 14 in. The wheel diameter on a two-wheel bandsaw determines the "throat" depth—the horizontal distance between the cutting blade and the body of the saw. A 14-in. Delta bandsaw has a 13¾-in. throat. The other significant measurement, the maximum width you can resaw, is determined by how high the upper guide unit lifts off the table. On a 14-in. bandsaw, this distance is just more than 6⅜ in.

Bandsaw blades

Bandsaw blades are distinguished by width, number of teeth per inch, and tooth shape. Narrower blades cut sharper curves; wider blades are better at cutting straight lines and resawing. A 14-in. bandsaw takes blades from 1/16 in. to ¾ in. in width, though ½ in. is the widest I find it necessary to use, even for resawing and cutting veneer.

Blades with fewer teeth cut thick stock better because they are more aggressively set, heat up less from friction, and carry dust out of the kerf more efficiently. Blades with more teeth per inch cut slower and leave a smoother surface. You have a lot of latitude in choosing the right blade for the job. Blade manufacturers go by a 3-6-12-24 rule. This means that there should be a minimum of 3 and a maximum of 24 teeth in contact with the wood at any given moment and that, preferably, there would be 6 to 12 teeth in contact. In other words, a 4-tooth blade would be

ideal for wood from 1½ in. to 3 in. thick but could be used on wood from ¾ in. to 6 in. thick.

There are two tooth forms used for woodcutting bandsaw blades: hook tooth and skip tooth. Hook teeth are more aggressive, remove a wider kerf, and are better for cutting hardwoods. Skip teeth have a larger gullet, clear chips better, and are preferred for cutting softwoods. Skip teeth cut more smoothly than hook teeth. For the record, I keep a four-tooth hook blade on my saw, changing to a six-tooth or eight-tooth hook only when I need a smoother cut or am working with thin stock.

SETTING THE DRIFT ON A BANDSAW

NLIKE THE TABLE SAW, much work on the bandsaw is done freehand, without fences or a miter gauge. When you do set up a fence, perhaps for resawing veneer from solid stock, there is an important trick to know called "setting the drift." A bandsaw blade rarely cuts in line with the edge of a bandsaw table. With the fence set parallel to the table (like a table-saw fence), the flexible blade tends to wander to one side until restrained by its own tension, slicing the wood either too thick or too thin.

To set the drift, mark a straight line parallel to the edge of a scrap board and then find the angle at which you must push the board through to saw along the line. This is the angle at which you should set the fence for perfect resawing.

1 Find the angle at which you must feed a board in order to saw along a line parallel to its edge.

2 Record the drift angle on a sliding T-bevel.

3 Set the fence to the recorded drift angle.

4 With the drift set correctly, you can accurately resaw boards as thin as you like, even cutting veneer.

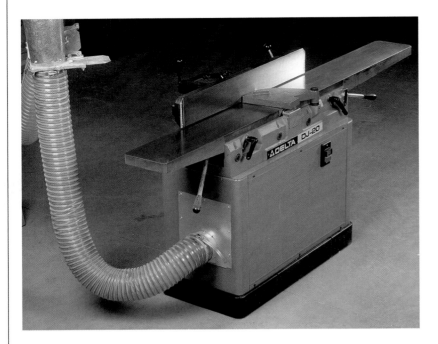

The jointer is used to establish a flat face and a perpendicular edge.

THE JOINTER

The jointer is used to make one face of a board flat and straight or one edge of a board flat, straight, and square to a face. It consists of two long, flat tables flanking a high-speed cylindrical cutterhead, a fence, a motor, and a blade guard. The cutterhead usually holds three parallel steel knives, though other configurations

are possible. Jointers are specified according to the length of their knives, which determines the width of board they can handle. Common sizes for home and small professional shops are 6 in. and 8 in. Wider is better—shops that handle timber for tabletops and cabinets may have jointers 18 in. wide and more.

The outfeed table of a jointer is set tangent to the apex of the knives' rotation (see the drawing below). The infeed table is set lower, determining the depth of cut. I take no more than ⅟₁₆ in. per pass so as not to strain the machine.

Wood should be fed through the jointer to cut with the grain as much as possible. If a board has grain running in two different directions, the best way to minimize tearout is to take fine cuts, make sure the knives are sharp, and feed the wood slowly.

"Snipe" is a common problem in jointed boards. It occurs when the outfeed table is set incorrectly. When the outfeed table is lower than the apex of the knives' rotation, the back end of a board gets cut slightly thinner than the rest. When it's too high, the front of the board becomes thinner. The length of snipe increases with each pass.

USING THE JOINTER

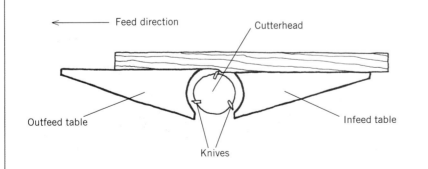

← Feed direction

Cutterhead

Outfeed table

Infeed table

Knives

TOOL TIP

When milling a gnarly piece of wood that will require many passes to become flat, I often disregard grain direction and flip the board end for end for the first several cuts. Flipping the board avoids the occasional problem of having more wood taken off one side of the board than the other by knives that are set unevenly in relation to the jointer tables. ■

The jointer may be the most demanding machine in the woodshop in terms of manufacturing quality control. Not only must each table be machined flat to within a few thousandths of an inch, but also both tables must be mounted so they are dead parallel. For example, if the infeed and outfeed tables tilt up and away from each other instead of being in parallel planes, boards will become convex.

The Thickness Planer

The thickness planer is used to make one face of a board parallel to the other face. Whereas a jointer's cutterhead lies in the same plane as its tables, a planer's cutterhead is above the table and wood passes between them. The planer's infeed roller, outfeed roller, and pressure bar force wood down on the table as it passes through the machine.

The only way to get flat, straight lumber out of a planer is to feed in boards that already have one flat, straight face to put down against the table as a reference. A cupped or bowed board, fed through a planer, may be flattened against the table by the rollers and pressure bar as it passes under the knives and then resume its warped shape as it exits the machine; it becomes a cupped or bowed board of uniform thickness. This is why surfaced boards from a lumberyard aren't ready for fine furniture. Lumberyards use only planers, not jointers, for surfacing wood—they make clean-faced boards of uniform thickness that aren't flat.

A thickness planer makes one face of a board parallel to the other.

The minimum-size planer used in small shops has knives 12 in. long. Larger shops may have planers with 20-in. or 30-in. knives. Thickness is set on some machines by raising or lowering the table. On other machines the cutterhead unit is moved up and down in relation to a stationary table. Some planers have variable-speed feed adjustments, which allow a slow feed for wood that threatens to tear out and a fast feed when you have to crank through a lot of board feet.

When a board is fed into a planer, the first thing that happens is that the corrugated infeed roller grabs the wood, presses it down, and pulls it along at a steady rate. Next, the board reaches the cutterhead and pressure bar. Then the smooth outfeed roller forces the wood even more firmly against the table and hastens it along.

The cutterhead is generally like the one on a jointer, with three straight steel knives spinning at high speed. It skims off the thickness of wood it has been set for, ideally no more than $\frac{1}{16}$ in. per pass. The pressure bar, which may be located just before or just after the cutterhead, keeps wood from chattering under the impact of the knives, which would create exaggerated parallel ridges across the board.

Many planers have two rollers set into the table bed to minimize friction. The problem with these table rollers is that they cause snipe by lifting the ends of a board off the table. As a general rule, keep table rollers set below the surface where they'll have no effect, and keep the table waxed (with paste wax) to minimize friction.

SAFETY TIPS
FOR THE THICKNESS PLANER

1 Never reach your hand into the cutterhead or under the infeed roller while the machine is operating.

2 If a board goes in awry, disengage the clutch (if your machine has one), turn off the machine, or lower the table.

3 Never run wood that might contain pieces of metal through a planer (or a jointer). The least that can happen is that your knives will be nicked. The worst is that shrapnel will fly.

4 Don't run pieces of wood through the planer that are less than 12 in. long.

USING THE THICKNESS PLANER

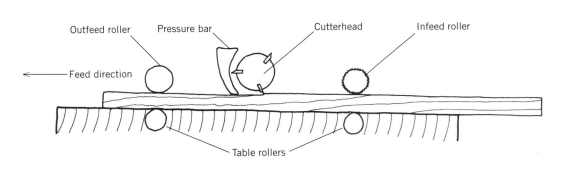

Outfeed roller Pressure bar Cutterhead Infeed roller

Feed direction

Table rollers

On a stationary-head planer, another cause of snipe is a loose planer table that rocks as a board passes through. This can be remedied by tightening the gib screws that hold the table to the body of the machine so that the table just barely slides up and down for height adjustment. Similarly, on a planer that has a moveable head and a fixed table, all play has to be adjusted out of the head.

THE DRILL PRESS

The drill press is used primarily to bore holes and provides the craftsman with more control than hand-held drills offer. Its main advantage is that it can bore holes consistently square to the table (or at any angle up to 45°). Its other virtue is a reliable depth-stop mechanism.

The speed at which a drill press turns is changed according to the material being bored and the diameter of the hole. Generally, metal should be bored at slower speeds than wood, and large holes should be bored at slower speeds than small ones. Some drill presses come with variable-speed adjustments as easy as turning a handle; others require that you manually move drive belts onto different arrangements of pulleys in order to change speed.

The drill press provides greater control than hand-held drills offer for boring holes.

SAFETY TIPS FOR THE DRILL PRESS

1 Always use the chuck key to tighten drill bits in place.

2 Never leave the chuck key inserted in the drill.

3 Before drilling small pieces of wood, clamp them to the table. They can be hard to hold by hand against the torque of the drill.

Usually, I place a piece of plywood or particleboard over the metal table of my drill press. Not only does this offer a larger work surface, but it also keeps me from accidentally dulling drill bits against the metal table.

THE RADIAL-ARM SAW

The radial-arm saw is essentially a large circular saw that is pulled along an overhead track. The arm can be raised or lowered to change the height of the blade relative to the table. The blade can also be angled to cut simple or compound miters. Saw size is specified by the diameter of the blade, which can range from 10 in. to 20 in. A popular size for small workshops takes a 12-in.-dia. blade. Radial-arm saw blades have their teeth set differently than blades used on table saws in order to diminish their tendency to "climb," or pull themselves through the wood.

Radial-arm saws can be used for crosscutting or ripping, but in my opinion ripping

TOOL TIP

A good way to improve a radial-arm saw is to build side-extension tables, with fences, to support long boards. When crosscutting, always hold wood firmly against the fence so it can't move and catch the sawblade. ■

on this saw is dangerous and impractical—a bandsaw or table saw should be used instead. The best use for a radial-arm saw is crosscutting rough lumber to approximate length at the start of the milling process. Radial-arm saws are too fickle for precise work because they don't maintain accurate settings. For the record, we don't bother to have a radial-arm saw in our school shop.

THE LATHE

The lathe is made to spin wood so it can be shaped with a variety of steel tools and abrasives. The essential components of a lathe are the bed, headstock, tailstock, tool rest, and motor. The headstock is stationary; the tailstock slides along the bed to accommodate spindle blanks of varying lengths.

By means of pulleys and a drive belt, the motor turns an arbor mounted horizontally through the headstock, which in turn drives the wood. Some lathes are variable speed; others require you to change speed by manually moving the drive belt onto different combinations of pulleys.

Two different types of work can be done with a lathe: spindle turning and faceplate turning. Spindle turning is used to make chair rungs, legs, candlesticks,

SAFETY TIPS FOR THE RADIAL-ARM SAW

1 Keep the blade sharp and free of pitch.

2 Never have your hand in the path of the blade.

3 Offer firm resistance against the travel of the blade while pulling it toward you; the blade will scream through anything in its way.

4 Never use the saw for ripping—it's just too dangerous.

LATHE ANATOMY

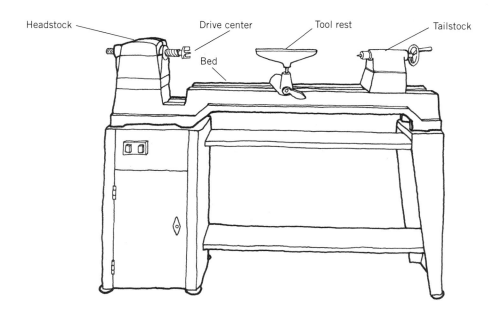

Headstock | Drive center | Tool rest | Tailstock
Bed

bedposts, and stair balusters. Wood is suspended lengthwise between the headstock and the tailstock. The headstock is fitted with a drive center to drive the wood; the tailstock is fitted with a simple centering pin or, preferably, a "live center," which rotates on a bearing.

Faceplate turning is used to make bowls, plates, and vases. A block of wood is screwed to a metal faceplate that attaches to the headstock. Large-diameter pieces can be turned by attaching the faceplate to the outside of the headstock and using a freestanding tool rest.

The hand tools used for spindle and faceplate turning include a variety of gouges, skew chisels, scrapers, and parting tools, usually with long handles for greater control. They are always used with a tool rest, never freehand.

Lathes are specified according to the maximum capacity between the headstock

SAFETY TIPS FOR THE LATHE

1 Always wear eye protection, preferably a face shield.

2 Make sure wood is held securely in the lathe. Before faceplate turning a large piece, get a head start by trimming it round on a bandsaw. Stand out of the way when starting up a lathe holding a large piece, in case the wood is so imbalanced that it flies off.

3 Keep a firm grip on the handle of the cutting tool so it can't flip up if the tip catches against the work.

and the tailstock, which defines the length available for spindle turning, and the distance from the bed to the center of the drive shaft, which is the radius available for inboard faceplate turning.

The standard lathe found in many home and small professional woodshops will handle wood approximately 39 in. in length for spindle turning and about 16 in. in diameter for inboard faceplate turning.

The five projects presented in this book do not require use of the lathe. For further information on this basic woodworking

machine, a good text is *Turning Wood with Richard Raffan* (The Taunton Press, 2001).

THE CHOPSAW

Although it is not one of the requisite tools in a furniture maker's shop, the chopsaw (properly called a miter saw) is a valuable auxiliary. It has a rotary blade that pivots onto a slotted table and, in some models, has a slide feature to give the blade greater reach. When accurately adjusted, chopsaws are good for cutting square or angled ends

THE CIRCULAR SAW

When it comes to cutting rough lumber to approximate length, the circular saw and the handsaw are the two most convenient choices, assuming you don't own a radial-arm saw.

To use a circular saw safely:

■ Place the board on sawhorses so that the location of the cut is just outside one of the supports. Never make a cut between two supports because the wood will bind on the blade as it drops.

■ Set the blade depth to slightly more than the thickness of the wood being cut.

■ Hold the wood steady with a foot or a knee (or clamps).

■ Be sure the blade isn't in contact with the wood when you turn the saw on.

■ Hold the saw with both hands, if possible.

■ Always push the saw forward——if you hesitate and start to retreat to straighten out a cut, the saw will often kick.

■ At the end of a cut, push quickly so the waste side falls off all at once, rather than splintering.

A circular saw is handy for cutting boards to rough length.

A chopsaw with side-extension tables is useful for making square or angled cuts on small stock.

rabbeting, grooving, and pattern shaping. Although considered essential equipment for a modern woodshop, the router is not a substitute for hand tools. For example, router-cut dovetails can't match the variety of spacings and angles, or the delicacy, that make hand-cut dovetails so seductive to the eye.

Essentially, a router is a hand-held motor that spins a cutting bit at speeds up to 26,000 rpm. The motor is mounted in a base that can be adjusted to vary the depth of cut. There are fixed-speed and variable-speed routers. Variable speed is not only more pleasant, because at slower speeds the machine is quieter, but also more practical: Larger-diameter router bits should be run at slower speeds.

A particularly useful accessory is a router table. The router is mounted upside down beneath the table with the bit protruding upward through a hole. This arrangement allows you to move the wood

on small-dimensioned stock. The chopsaw at the Center for Furniture Craftsmanship has a 12-in.-dia. blade that will make square cuts across wood up to 8 in. wide and 5½ in. thick.

Enhance the utility of a chopsaw by building side-extension tables to support long boards. Always hold wood firmly against the fence. Don't cut pieces of wood less than 5 in. to 6 in. long; they can be difficult to hold securely without putting your fingers in jeopardy.

The Router

Routers perform a wide variety of woodworking operations, including edge shaping, flush trimming, mortising, dovetailing,

Routers are useful for a wide variety of woodworking operations, including edge shaping, flush trimming, and mortising.

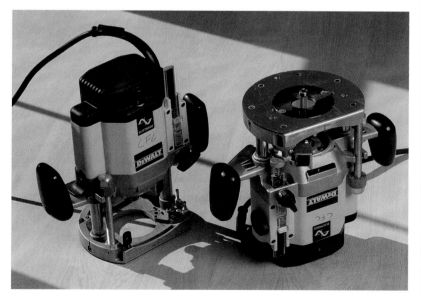

A table-mounted router often allows greater control than a hand-held router.

against a stationary bit, rather than the other way around.

These days, most routers have a plunge feature that allows the bit to be lowered and raised through the base while the machine is running. This is a particularly useful feature for making mortises (see pp. 166–167) and for grooves that are stopped at one or both ends.

Routers are specified according to collet size and horsepower. The collet (see the sidebar on the facing page) is the sleeve that receives the shank of the bit. Routers generally come with ¼-in. and/or ½-in. collet capacities. Because bits with thicker shanks vibrate less, larger collet capacity is an advantage when working with large cutters.

SAFETY TIPS FOR THE ROUTER

EVEN THOUGH THE ROUTER is a small machine, it demands the same safety consciousness as do larger ones. Safety tips for the router include:

1 Always wear eye and ear protection.

2 Always unplug the router before changing bits.

3 Start with a light cut and extend the bit a little farther on successive passes, rather than trying to remove too much wood at one time. Otherwise you may strain the motor or burn the bit.

4 Keep firm control of the router at all times.

5 When shaping an edge, move the router against the rotation of the cutter so the router doesn't pull itself along.

6 When working on a router table, never have your hand in a position where it could suddenly be drawn into the cutter if the bit were to grab the wood. Be sure to feed wood against the rotation of the cutter.

CHANGING ROUTER BITS

A router bit fits into a collet, which is held, in turn, within an opening on the end of the motor shaft. The collet is a metal sleeve with slits cut along its length. When a bit is installed, the pressure exerted by turning a threaded nut causes the collet to close tightly around the bit and simultaneously forces the collet into a friction fit within the motor-shaft opening. When you change bits, remove the collet and clean out any dust that may have collected around it.

Most modern routers have safety collets designed to retain a bit even if the collet works loose. To remove a bit, loosen the collet with a wrench, then unscrew it freely until you get to a second tight spot where you must use the wrench again.

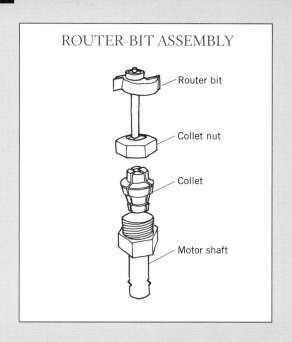

ROUTER-BIT ASSEMBLY

Router bit

Collet nut

Collet

Motor shaft

Router motors range from ½ hp up to 3 hp. A commercial cabinet shop needs the brute strength of a 3-hp router, but most furniture makers can easily get by with less horsepower and, consequently, less noise. If I had to have only one router, it would be a 1½ hp, variable-speed plunge router that took both ¼-in. and ½-in. collets.

Cutting bits for routers have edges of high-speed steel or carbide. Carbide is more expensive but stays sharp so much longer that it's worth the cost. Edge-profile, flush-trim, and rabbet bits generally have bearings attached that serve as fences.

THE SHAPER

The shaper is a larger, more powerful version of a router table and is used primarily for edge profiles, tongue-and-groove joinery, moldings, raised panels, and pattern shaping. It is indispensable for commercial production but not at all necessary for making one-of-a-kind fine furniture.

Many consider the shaper to be the most dangerous woodworking machine in the workshop. The use of shapers is not covered in this book.

THE GRINDER

Electric grinders are used in the sharpening process to restore hollow bevels to chisels and plane irons (see pp. 72–74). They are also good for reshaping screwdriver tips and performing other metal-grinding tasks that come up from time to time. There are two basic types of grinders. One is the high-speed machinists' bench grinder, which rotates 6-in.-dia., 7-in.-dia., or 8-in.-dia. abrasive wheels at speeds ranging from 1,500 rpm to 3,600 rpm. The other is the slow-speed, water-cooled grinder, which typically has a 10-in.-dia. abrasive wheel running at 90 rpm.

Of the two, machinist's bench grinders are far more efficient, but the friction of high-speed grinding can "burn" steel, that is, heat it to the point where it loses its temper—its hardness—and won't hold a sharp edge. For this reason, we use 6-in. bench grinders that run at 1,800 rpm rather than the standard 3,600 rpm. In addition, we have replaced the original gray aluminum-oxide grinding wheels with softer white aluminum-oxide wheels. White wheels cut faster, with less friction, because they have a softer binder that wears away to expose fresh abrasive particles. Gray wheels cut more slowly, creating more heat.

When the surface of a grinding wheel clogs with steel or wears unevenly, it is trued up with a diamond-point dresser or a coarse aluminum-oxide dressing stick.

A 1,800 rpm machinist's bench grinder with a white aluminum-oxide wheel is less likely to burn steel than the standard model.

Common electric sanders include (clockwise from top left) a 4-in. disk grinder, a palm sander, a belt sander, and a random-orbital disk sander.

SANDERS

The two ways to work wood are to cut it or abrade it. Mastery of the hand skills involved in cutting (with saws, chisels, planes, scrapers, spokeshaves, and so on) requires more patience and practice than working with abrasives does, but cutting also provides more control and better results. I do relatively little sanding and that mostly by hand. I don't care for the noise and dust generated by electric sanders.

My prejudices aside, sanders are useful. They are commonly employed to flatten surfaces, fair curves, shape forms, round edges, and smooth wood preparatory to finishing.

Sandpaper works by abrasion and leaves scratches behind. The finer the grit, the smaller the scratches. The smaller the

scratches, the greater depth-of-grain the finished wood will appear to have. When I sand a tabletop with 150-grit paper, I sand until the entire surface is uniformly abraded and I have removed any tears, nicks, or scratches deeper than those created by the sandpaper. Then I sand the entire surface with 220-grit paper to remove the scratches left by the 150-grit paper. If I were to keep going with finer and finer grits, I would eventually achieve a polished surface disturbed only by the pores of the wood.

Sanders can be distinguished from one another by their motions: There are sanders that move a belt in a continuous loop, sanders that spin a disk, sanders that rotate a cylinder, and sanders that move a sheet of sandpaper in an orbital motion. Brief descriptions follow.

Belt sanders

Hand-held belt sanders take continuous, replaceable belts of sandpaper. Most commonly, belts measure 3 in. or 4 in. in width and 20 in. or 24 in. in circumference. Belt sanders are used primarily to flatten and smooth large surfaces like tabletops. They remove wood so quickly that they are difficult to control and are prone to create ridges and depressions.

Stationary belt sanders often have larger belts that are used to flatten small surfaces and to round and smooth convex curves.

A stroke sander has a large belt, generally about 6 in. wide by 25 ft. in circumference, suspended between rollers above a table that slides forward and back. The spinning belt is stroked against a piece of wood with a hand-held platen from inside the loop. Stroke sanders are used in production shops for sanding large, flat surfaces.

"Time-savers" are stationary belt sanders that work like thickness planers. In place of a single cutterhead, they have one, two, or three belts that loop around rollers set above the table. Each consecutive belt spins a finer grit of sandpaper. At first, time-savers were found only in large production shops. Now smaller, less expensive versions are gaining in popularity.

Disk sanders

Hand-held disk sanders, also called grinders, take disks of sandpaper ranging from about 4 in. to 9 in. in diameter. They are primarily metalworking tools but are excellent for removing lots of wood quickly when sculpting forms. The circular motion of disk sanders makes it impossible to sand with the grain—they always leave cross-grain scratches.

Stationary units have disks ranging from 6 in. to 20 in. in diameter that work in reference to tables. They are useful for flattening small pieces of wood and the ends of butt joints, for forming and smoothing convex curves, and for odds and ends of metalwork that come up from time to time. Material should be sanded only on the side of the disk that spins down toward the table; the rising side can throw work in your face.

Drum sanders

Stationary drum sanders spin a horizontal or vertical cylindrical drum that is fitted with a cylindrical sanding sleeve. Drums come in a wide variety of diameters and lengths. Some are solid rubber, whereas some are air-filled. They are used for shaping and smoothing concave and convex surfaces and for rounding edges.

Orbital sanders

The palm sander is the least aggressive of sanders and works well for the craftsman making fine furniture. This small sander takes only a quarter-sheet of sandpaper. It

BUYING MACHINERY

Buying woodworking machines is much like buying anything else—you get what you pay for. Don't try to save money by purchasing cheap equipment. Rickety frames, underpowered motors, and moving parts machined to poor tolerances add up to frustrating hours of work and bad results.

The best way to find out which machines are worth buying is to ask professional woodworkers who use them all the time, rather than salespeople. You'll be a lot more likely to get reliable information based on experience.

Even when buying a new machine made by a reputable manufacturer, there are some things to look out for:

- Use a good straightedge to make sure tables are flat to within a few thousandths of an inch, especially on jointers. Also, check to see that jointer tables are parallel to each other

and that the fence isn't twisted along its length.

- Look for runout in the spindles of boring machines, table saws, and shapers. Runout, the degree to which a shaft spins eccentrically on its axis, should be less than 0.0005 in. on a table-saw arbor. A reputable machine dealer will measure runout for you.

- Don't buy machines before you really need them. Purchase machinery only when you understand what it does and what you need it for, unless you are on a limitless budget.

Machines can't make you into an excellent craftsman; only practice and a willingness to master hand skills can do that. But machines can be a help and a time-saver for the craftsman who knows how they fit into the overall process.

---

is stroked in the direction of the grain and vibrates in small swirls, removing wood quite controllably. At the finer grits, the swirls become virtually invisible. Palm sanders are used for surface smoothing of flat and curved shapes.

Half-sheet orbital sanders, a larger form of the palm sander, are more useful on flat surfaces and less useful on curved ones.

Random-orbital disk sanders

The random-orbital disk sander is the best choice for most surface preparation applications in the woodshop. It unites the spin of a disk sander with the swirl of an orbital sander. This makes it reasonably aggressive, yet it leaves little behind in the way of cross-grain scratches.

Introduction to
Hand Tools

THE MAN-MADE DEVICES that augment our bare hands in working wood can be divided into two classes: hand-driven tools and power-driven tools. Hand tools are to power tools what walking is to driving. Walking will get you just about anywhere. From urban back alleys to mountain meadows radiant with lupine and larkspur—you can walk as far off the "beaten path" as your heart desires. Walking immerses you in the environment; you trace the cragginess of pine bark with a fingertip, hear the splash of a trout, smell the air change as rain comes on.

Driving limits the choice of destination to places where roads already go; places accessible to anyone, anytime. You directly experience only the plastic, vinyl, and glass of your car's interior. The natural environment passes behind the windshield as distant as a video on a television screen. Walking is about the journey; driving is about the destination.

Like walking, hand tools open an infinite range of form, surface texture, and detail to the furniture maker. Handwork provides a depth of experience that power tools cannot. For example, when I smooth a tabletop with a jack plane instead of an electric sander, I hear the snick of the razor-sharp blade gliding through cherry, see the transparency of the shavings, and feel the sole of the plane as it reveals each minute knoll and dip. With a sander, I experience only vibration, loud noise, and dust.

The direct connection between a tool and the finely tuned nerves and muscles of your hands gives you direct experience of a piece of wood in all its quirky character. With power tools, one board seems little different from another. Nothing happens except as you make it happen with hand tools. Your control is as complete as your skill.

You might ask, "Does Korn ever get in a car, or does he walk everywhere?" Rest assured! When I lived in Colorado and wanted to see mountain wildflowers I didn't walk the 27 miles from my house to the trailhead; I drove. Then, on foot, I climbed 2,000 vertical feet of narrow, rocky footpaths to high alpine meadows most people will never see. In the same way, I use a table saw, jointer, planer, and bandsaw to rough out and thickness the parts of a stool. Then, with hand tools, I cut the joinery, fair the curves, and smooth the surfaces.

The raw truth about hand tools, though, is that most are just tool kits at the time of purchase—they don't work worth a damn until they've been tuned and sharpened. This particularly applies to planes, chisels, saws, cutting gauges, and scrapers. For more detailed information on selecting, tuning, and using hand tools than I could fit within the confines of this chapter, I refer you to my book *The Woodworker's Guide to Hand Tools* (The Taunton Press, 1998).

What follows are descriptions of the furniture maker's essential hand tools.

THE WORKBENCH

The workbench is the single most important tool in the woodshop. It should be flat on top, strong enough to take a pounding, and sturdy enough not to wobble.

A traditional European workbench generally incorporates a face vise and a tail vise. The face vise (see the bottom photo below) holds wood against the edge of the bench. It is indispensable in hundreds of woodworking operations, such as marking and sawing joinery or handplaning an edge.

This European-style workbench, manufactured by Ulmia, incorporates a face vise, a tail vise, and a tool tray.

A face vise holds wood against the edge of the workbench.

A tail vise is used with bench dogs to hold wood flat upon the workbench.

The tail vise (see the top photo at left) mounts on the end of the workbench. Rectangular holes in the tail vise line up with a series of rectangular holes running the length of the top. Wood is held flat on the bench between a bench dog inserted into the tail vise and a bench dog inserted into the benchtop. Because bench dogs offer no obstruction, this setup is ideal for face planing.

The functions of face and tail vises are sometimes combined in a metal bench vise (see the bottom photo at left), which is essentially a face vise that incorporates a dog. Mounted at the end of a workbench, it does the work of both vises.

Metalworking vises are also extremely useful for woodworking, especially when fitted with wooden jaws to protect the work. They hold wood above the plane of the benchtop and can be mounted on a separate table.

A metal bench vise (with auxiliary wooden jaws) combines the functions of the tail vise and the face vise.

TOOL TIP

Whether your workbench is a $1,500 imported European beechwood model or homemade out of particleboard, it deserves to be treated with the same respect as any other tool in your shop. If you are going to drill or chisel through a board on the bench's surface, place scrap wood underneath to protect the benchtop. If you use your bench for glue-ups, cover the surface (with paper, plastic, tempered hardboard...) to catch any squeezed-out glue. ■

FOLDING RULE

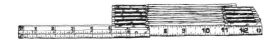

MEASURING TOOLS

The tradesman's traditional measuring tool, the folding wooden rule, has been supplanted over the past 50 years by the tape measure. I find both tools useful.

TAPE MEASURES are the handier choice when selecting and milling lumber. Because hardwood boards rarely come in lengths greater than 12 ft., a 16-ft. tape is sufficient. For the more exacting work of marking joinery and fitting, I prefer a folding rule. It is easier to handle, doesn't flex, and stays where I lay it. Both Lufkin and Starrett make superior folding rules with extension slides, which are particularly handy for taking inside measurements and for checking hole depths.

SQUARES, STRAIGHTEDGES, AND T-BEVELS

Squares are used to make sure things are at right angles to one another. In a woodshop, these things might be the edge of a board, the shoulder of a tenon, the fence on a jointer, the end of a chisel, the sides of a drawer, the leg of a chair, and so on.

Square is an abstract term. Looked at closely enough, nothing is truly square; some things just approach the ideal more than others. In general, squares manufac-

tured for woodworking aren't made to the strict tolerances of squares made for machinists. However, even for the woodworker it doesn't hurt to have the squarest square you can find. There are four types of squares that I find useful: combination squares, try squares or engineer's squares, double squares, and framing squares.

COMBINATION SQUARES are designed to mark both 90° and 45° angles. A top-quality combination square, such as one made by Starrett, is excellent for accurate layout and joinery, as well as for machine tuning and setups. It was years before I could afford one of these squares, but now that I have one I would never want to build furniture without it.

TRY SQUARES are the traditional tool of furniture makers. They have blades of

TWO SQUARES

Combination
square

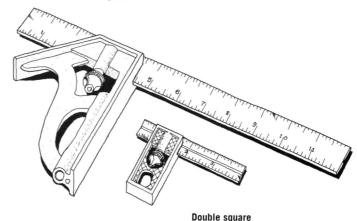

Double square

TRY SQUARE

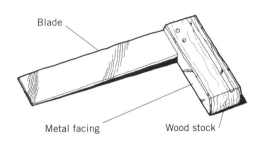

Blade

Metal facing

Wood stock

brass or steel (generally from 6 in. to 12 in. long) and wood fences that are usually faced with metal to ensure long-term accuracy. **ENGINEER'S SQUARES** are similar in design to try squares but made entirely of steel, and can be used interchangeably with them in the woodshop. Blade lengths start at about 2 in.

The reliability of try squares and engineer's squares can vary sharply, even among those made by the same manufacturer. At the Center for Furniture Craftsmanship, we often have to return squares our students have bought because they are too inaccurate. The only sure way to buy a square is to pick it out yourself or order it from one of the few makers who guarantee accuracy to extremely close tolerances.

A 4-in. **DOUBLE SQUARE** is incredibly handy for joinery, installing hardware, and many other daily tasks. The sliding blade increases its versatility.

FRAMING SQUARES are made for house building. They have two large blades that form a right angle. One blade is 2 in. wide by 24 in. long; the other is 1½ in. by 18 in. long. Framing squares are not expected to be as precise as the other squares listed in this section. I find them useful when building large cabinets, cutting rough lumber to approximate length, or doing carpentry.

STRAIGHTEDGES can be made of metal, wood, or plastic. Their uses include checking the flatness of boards, drawing straight lines, and setting up machinery. I have a variety of lengths hanging in the shop, from 12 in. to 48 in. When I need a longer straightedge, I often use an 8-ft. scrap of medium-density fiberboard (MDF).

A flexible metal straightedge is also useful for drawing fair curves. When making full-scale drawings of curved parts, I often flex a metal rule between my hands and, if no one is there to help, trace the curve with a pencil held between my teeth.

The **SLIDING T-BEVEL** is used to transfer and mark angles. Metal-bodied T-bevels generally have more reliably straight shoulders than do wooden ones. The best locking mechanism for the blade is a thumbscrew at the base, where it's out of

TOOL TIP

If you are selecting a square in person, check it against one of the reliable machinists' squares that the tool store is likely to have on hand, such as a Starrett combination square. ∎

SLIDING T-BEVEL

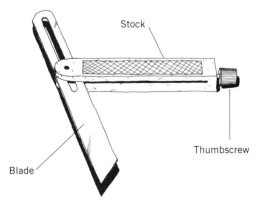

Stock

Thumbscrew

Blade

the way, rather than a wing nut at the pivot point, which can hold the fence off the work in certain positions.

MARKING TOOLS

Pencils love to play hide and seek. One minute a pencil is behind your ear, and the next it has disappeared without a trace. Even though we play this game many times a day, the pencil never seems to get bored.

Ordinary, school-type **PENCILS** are useful for marking wood in order to keep track of jointed surfaces, how pieces fit together, and where machine cuts should be made. I also like china markers and Prismacolor pencils for their bold, unmistakable markings. But the most indispensable pencil in my shop is a **LEAD HOLDER** made for drafting. Lead holders are ideal for marking out joints, as well as for drafting and drawing, because they take a much finer point than a school pencil, and a precise line can be crucial to accurate joinery.

Leads come in a range of hardness from 6B (softest) to 6H (hardest). Harder lead makes a fainter line but holds a point longer. I use an H or 2H lead to mark out joinery.

KNIVES are indispensable in a woodshop for tasks as varied as marking tenon shoulders and cutting cardboard templates. I've

---

MORTISING GAUGE

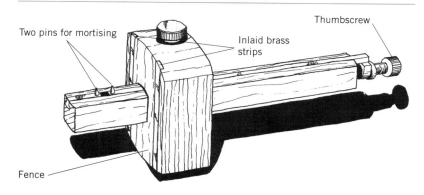

Two pins for mortising · Inlaid brass strips · Thumbscrew · Fence

---

seen woodworkers use almost every kind of knife successfully, from a Boy Scout penknife to a reground file. My personal preference is a common utility knife with replaceable blades that can be bought at any hardware store.

AWLS are sharp, pointed instruments with a variety of uses. They differ in the fineness of their points and the thickness of their shafts. A fine-pointed awl is useful for marking out joinery and scribing lines (though I find a pencil line easier to read on all but dark woods). A thick-shanked, broad-pointed awl (see the drawing at left) is good for making pilot marks in wood prior to drilling. The dimple it leaves when tapped with a mallet forms an exact starting point for a drill bit.

Marking and mortise gauges are used to lay out joinery. A **MARKING GAUGE** incorporates a single pin and an adjustable fence for scribing a line parallel to an edge. A **MORTISE GAUGE** is similar, except that it has two pins that can be adjusted in relation to one another and scribes a double line. Marking and mortise gauges can be bought as separate tools, but you're more likely to find their functions combined in a **COMBINATION GAUGE**.

AWL

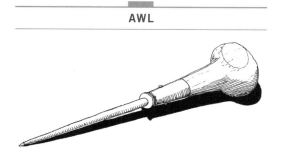

A **CUTTING GAUGE** looks like a marking gauge, except that in place of a pin it has a small blade sharpened to cut like a knife. It is particularly useful for precise marking across grain, as when laying out dovetail shoulders. Knife blades are always preferable for cross-grain marking because they slice wood fibers cleanly where a pin tends to tear.

SAWS

The projects in this book call for the furniture maker's most commonly used saws—a dovetail saw, a coping saw, and perhaps a handsaw.

The **DOVETAIL SAW** is a form of backsaw, a family of saws whose blades are stiffened with metal spines. Dovetail saws vary according to handle design, blade length and thickness, number of teeth per inch, and the shape of the teeth. The saw I currently use is an inexpensive Stanley dovetail saw with 15 teeth per inch. It cost only $12.50, but once I've sharpened it, it's as good as any Western-style saw on the market. However, there is another type of dovetail saw that many furniture makers swear by. This is the Japanese dozuki saw,

DOVETAIL SAW

COPING SAW

which works on the pull stroke and gives an amazingly fine, precise cut.

A **COPING SAW** cuts curves and can also cut interior shapes out of a board. When making dovetails, I use a coping saw to remove the waste wood between the pins or the tails.

To saw an interior shape, drill a hole through the waste wood, take the coping saw apart, stick the blade through the hole, and reassemble the saw around the blade. A coping saw cannot cut farther in from the wood's edge than the distance between the sawblade and the saw frame. Coping-saw blades come in packages of five or more—when one breaks or gets dull you throw it away and install another.

Most applications of the **HANDSAW** are now fulfilled by power tools, but I still find handsawing a pleasant way to cut boards to rough length at the start of the milling process. The teeth of handsaws are shaped for either crosscutting or ripping. A saw with more teeth per inch leaves a smoother surface but cuts more slowly.

DRILLS

As grateful as I am for the utility and convenience of electric drills, there are still

HANDSAW

DRILL BITS

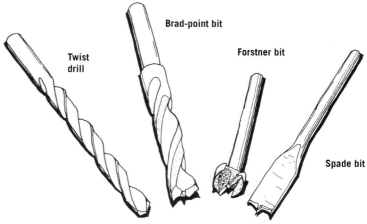

Twist drill

Brad-point bit

Forstner bit

Spade bit

times when a hand drill is preferable: to drill in a tight space; for increased control; or for the simple pleasure of using a quieter, lighter tool. Two types of hand drill are the egg beater and the brace.

Drill bits

The drill bits found in a woodshop include twist drills, brad-point bits, Forstner bits, and spade bits. Each has distinct advantages and limitations.

TWIST DRILLS will make holes in wood, metal, plastic, and just about any other

HAND DRILLS

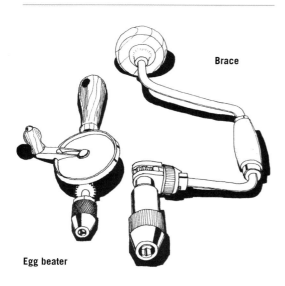

Brace

Egg beater

material. They are a necessary item for the woodworker because of their versatility and their great range of closely graduated diameters (from ⅟₁₆ in. to 1 in. by sixty-fourths). The disadvantages of twist drills for furniture making are twofold: They are difficult to center perfectly and tend to walk before establishing a location, and they often drill holes that are slightly elliptical.

BRAD-POINT BITS have center spurs that engage wood before the cutting edge makes contact, so holes are exactly placed and perfectly round. Commonly available in sizes from ⅛ in. to ½ in. by sixteenths, and from ½ in. to 1 in. by eighths, brad points are generally the best bits for woodworking, although they are useless for drilling metal.

In those rare situations where a hole goes so deep that the protruding spur of a brad point would poke through to the other side, a **FORSTNER BIT** can be used. The center spurs of Forstner bits are practically flush with the cutters, so they make extremely clean, flat-bottomed holes. Also, because they center themselves on their rims,

Forstner bits can drill over existing holes or take a half-moon shape out of the edge of a (well-clamped) board—things a brad point could never to. The downside of Forstner bits is that they cut slowly and heat up fast.

SPADE BITS are really carpentry tools, useful for chasing pipes through framing but not much good for accurate work in hardwoods. They tend to overheat, cut slowly, and make rough, inaccurate holes.

CHISELS

The chopping and paring abilities of chisels make them useful in so many ways that scarcely a day goes by that the furniture maker doesn't use one. They are essential to hand cutting and fitting of joinery, especially mortise-and-tenon joints and dovetails.

There are three main families of chisels: firmer, paring, and mortise. **FIRMER CHISELS** are durably made to take on any job. **PARING CHISELS** are lighter in construction and meant only for paring under hand control rather than for chopping under a mallet. **MORTISE CHISELS** are specialized for the heavy work of chopping mortises.

CHISELS

Mortise chisel

Firmer chisel

The first (and, really, only) set of chisels a furniture maker needs are bevel-edged firmer chisels in widths of ¼ in., ⅜ in., ½ in., ¾ in., and 1 in. I use standard Western-style chisels, but Japanese-style chisels with bi-metal blades can be superb. I also have a few mortise chisels (¼ in., ⁵⁄₁₆ in., ⅜ in., and ½ in.) but for many years got by perfectly well without them. I find no need for paring chisels in my workshop.

Chisels vary in worth according to the steel in their blades and the durability of their handles. The quality and temper of the steel are of first importance. Steel that is too soft or too brittle won't hold a sharp edge. Blades that are too thin may bend in use or warp from the heat of grinding.

A chisel handle that is badly made or poorly attached won't hold up under serious use. Good-quality wooden handles should take a pounding without splitting, but I'm content with durable plastic handles.

Leave your chisels sharp at the end of each day's work. It is a great pleasure to reach into your tool cabinet and pull out a chisel sharp enough to shave hair, rather than interrupt the flow of work with a dull blade. Detailed instructions for sharpening chisels are given on pp. 72–76.

Mallets

Wooden mallets, metal hammers, dead-blow mallets, and rubber mallets are the four striking implements generally found in a woodshop. Of the four, wooden mallets are best for driving chisels. They deliver firm impact with minimum damage to the chisel handle. A metal hammer would be too destructive, and the impact of a dead-blow or rubber mallet is too cushioned to be effective.

Wooden mallets come in two styles. **CARPENTER'S MALLETS** have a rectilinear head mounted at right angles to a shaft. **CARVER'S MALLETS** are cylindrical and usually turned from a single piece of wood. I prefer the balance of a carver's mallet, but either works just fine. Mallets come in a variety of weights. The right weight for you is whatever you find effective and comfortable.

Deadblow and rubber mallets are best for fitting joints or knocking furniture together during glue-ups. They are the least likely to dent wood. If glue has begun to set and a joint gets stubborn, I switch to a steel hammer for greater impact but interpose a piece of scrap wood to avoid dents.

Planes

The basic planes for furniture making are bench planes and block planes, which are used to flatten and smooth wood surfaces. Scrub planes are also useful in the initial stages of flattening a board. A wide variety of specialty planes exists for cleaning shoul-

WOODEN MALLETS

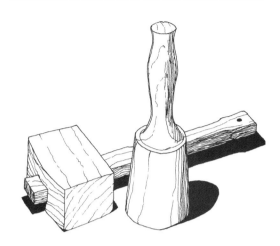

ders, rabbeting, and molding edges, among other things. The four plane types I find most useful are listed on the next page.

BENCH PLANES generally come in lengths from 9 in. to 24 in. The longer the plane, the flatter the surface it leaves. Where a straight, square edge is needed for gluing one board to another, you might use a 24-in. jointer plane. A 9-in. smoothing plane, on the other hand, would be used to clean small defects from an already flattened surface. If I could have

PLANES

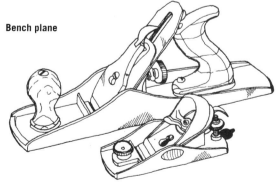

Bench plane

Block plane

only one plane for all-around use, it would be a 14-in. jack plane.

BLOCK PLANES are shorter than bench planes, usually about 6 in. long. Their blades are set at a lower angle to minimize tearout when planing end grain. I use a block plane to flatten end-grain surfaces, make dovetails and through tenons flush after glue-up, chamfer edges, and smooth convex surfaces.

SCRUB PLANES are flat-bottomed planes with convex cutting edges. They are moved across the grain to flatten rough lumber quickly. Pushed along the grain, scrub planes can make nasty tearouts.

SHOULDER PLANES are used primarily to clean up the shoulders and cheeks of tenons. The sides of a shoulder plane are machined square to the sole, and the blade is the full width of the body.

Other types of plane that we find particularly useful at the Center for Furniture Craftsmanship include spokeshaves, router planes, and scratchstocks.

Until the 19th century, all planes were wood-bodied, with wooden wedges to hold the irons in place. Depth of cut and blade angle were adjusted by tapping the iron with a hammer. Today, most commercially available planes are made of metal, with mechanical blade adjustments. But

SHOULDER PLANE

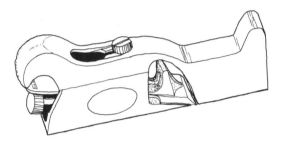

both types of planes are equally useful and there is great pleasure, as well as utility, in making your own wooden handplanes for special requirements.

SPOKESHAVES

A spokeshave is a type of plane used primarily to round edges, make spindles, and fair concave curves. The short sole of a spokeshave is mounted between two handles. The blade is generally held in place with a cap iron. Spokeshaves can be used with either a pulling or a pushing motion.

Spokeshaves are made with flat, convex, or concave soles. For general use, a flat sole is sufficient.

SCRUB PLANE

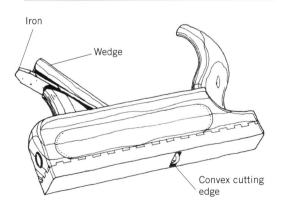

Iron

Wedge

Convex cutting edge

TUNING UP A PLANE

The key to using any plane is in tuning it up. Bench and block planes should have flat soles, but very few come that way from the manufacturer. Whenever you get a new plane, plan to spend a few hours abrading the bottom flat. A good method is to use 100-grit pressure-sensitive adhesive (psa) sandpaper on a long, flat surface such as a jointer table.

The second major requirement of a well-tuned plane is that the blade (iron) be razor sharp, with the bevel ground to 25° to 30°. (Detailed instructions for sharpening plane blades are given on pp. 72–76.) If you find yourself wondering whether the blade in a particular plane should be inserted bevel up or bevel down, remember that manufacturers want their names to be visible at all times. The side on which the name is engraved faces up.

The size of the throat—the space where shavings pass between the blade and the sole—should be experimented with for optimum performance. Throat size is controlled on a metal bench plane by sliding the frog forward or back. Generally, throat size is increased to take coarser shavings when flattening

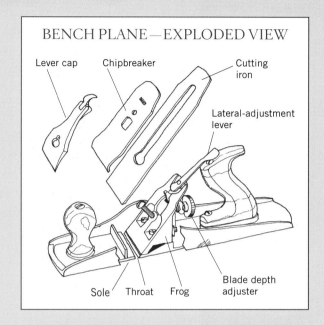

BENCH PLANE—EXPLODED VIEW

Lever cap   Chipbreaker   Cutting iron

Lateral-adjustment lever

Blade depth adjuster

Sole   Throat   Frog

rough boards, and decreased to take fine shavings and reduce tearout during final smoothing.

The chipbreaker should be set close to the cutting edge of the blade—within about $\frac{1}{32}$ in. This part of the plane breaks shavings to keep them from tearing out ahead of the blade. It also stiffens the iron to reduce chattering.

SCRAPERS AND BURNISHERS

When I was a 22-year-old, inexperienced house carpenter, I went to Spain. Under a makeshift awning at a dusty hillside market, an old man was selling his woodworking tools. As I watched, he drew sinuous shavings from a board with only a thin, flat piece of metal between his hands.

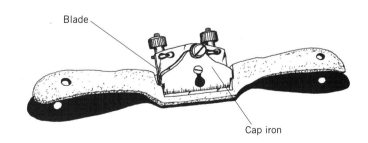

SPOKESHAVE

Blade

Cap iron

I imagined I was witnessing a secret of ancient craftsmanship that he would take to his grave. But I was too shy to ask questions, so it was several more years before I learned that his magic was a common hand scraper.

A **HAND SCRAPER** (or card scraper) is a thin, flat piece of moderately hard steel, about 3 in. wide and 6 in. long. When the edge is burnished—stroked with a harder piece of steel—it rolls over into a barely perceptible, wood-cutting hook. A properly sharpened hand scraper takes shavings without tearout, even working against the grain.

Scrapers are used primarily to smooth surfaces prior to sanding and finishing. Not all scrapers are straight-edged. Curved scrapers are used to smooth forms that are curved in section. Scrapers can be cut and filed to special shapes for individual jobs.

Although the hand scraper is the simplest tool in the woodshop, it is, paradoxically, one of the most difficult to master. Instructions are given on pp. 140–141.

HAND SCRAPER

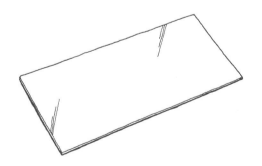

CABINET SCRAPER

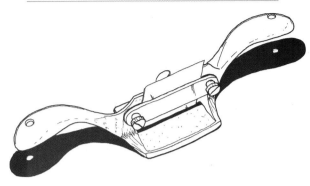

A **CABINET SCRAPER** holds a scraper blade so that its cutting action is directed by the sole of the tool. Although it tends to leave a coarser surface than a hand scraper does, the cabinet scraper is more comfortable to hold and more aggressive. It is particularly useful for flattening and smoothing boards that resist planing due to interlocking grain. In general, though, I find a hand scraper to be the more versatile, useful tool and rarely have recourse to a cabinet scraper.

BURNISHERS are smooth rods of hard steel used to put an edge on a scraper. They can be round, oval, teardrop, or triangular in section. The more highly polished a burnisher is, the smoother and sharper the edge it imparts to the scraper will be.

Files and Rasps

Wood files and rasps are used primarily to shape edges, form curves, and sculpt wood. **FILES** are lengths of hard steel whose surfaces have been scored with raised ridges in parallel patterns. The depth of the scoring and the nature of the pattern determine the degree of abrasiveness. Files come in a variety of shapes including flat, half-round (flat on one side and rounded on the other), round, and triangular. A good, all-purpose file for woodworking is a 10-in. half-round "wood" or "cabinet" file. For flattening scrapers and other metal filing tasks, an 8-in. mill file is handy.

RASPS are lengths of hard steel on which small teeth have been raised. Less expensive wood rasps have teeth in regular patterns. They leave a rougher surface than the more expensive patternmaker's rasps, whose teeth are raised in random patterns. My first choice of rasp would be a #49 patternmaker's rasp, which removes wood quickly but relatively cleanly.

CLAMPS

Clamps are used to squeeze pieces of wood together, particularly during assembly and gluing. The major varieties are bar clamps, pipe clamps, quick-action clamps, C-clamps, hand screws, band clamps, and spring clamps.

A **BAR CLAMP** consists of two jaws mounted on a length of steel bar, often I-shaped in section. One jaw is fixed, the other slides along the bar, and tightening is accomplished with a screw-thread and handle. A **PIPE CLAMP** is similar except that it substitutes pipe for bar and is consequently less rigid. Of the two, bar clamps are best for assembling wide surfaces, such as tabletops, and for putting together large carcases.

QUICK-ACTION CLAMPS have a fixed jaw at one end of a flat steel bar. A second jaw, which incorporates a screw-thread and handle, slides on the bar to fix in any posi-

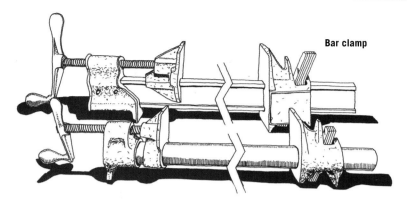

BAR AND PIPE CLAMPS

Bar clamp

Pipe clamp

tion. Quick-action clamps come in a range of sizes from 4-in. to 60-in. maximum open span between the jaws.

Besides length, the two variables in quick-action clamps are throat depth and bar size. Throat depth (the distance from the tip of the jaws to the bar) limits the distance the clamp will reach in from the edge of a board. Bar size relates to strength—a clamp with a thicker bar exerts more pressure with less flex.

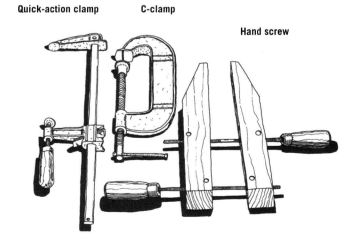

OTHER WOODWORKING CLAMPS

Quick-action clamp   C-clamp

Hand screw

Quick-action clamps are the workhorse among clamps. They are constantly in use for holding work on a bench, improvising fences on machinery, clamping bent laminations, assembling chairs and small carcases, and countless other tasks.

C-CLAMPS have a C-shaped metal body with a screw-thread and handle entering at one end. Like other clamps, they come in a wide variety of lengths, throat depths, and bar thicknesses. C-clamps can be used interchangeably with quick-action clamps, though in many situations they are more cumbersome.

HAND SCREWS have wooden jaws that are moved together or apart by means of wooden or metal screw-threads. They may look antique but are in fact quite useful. The jaws, being wood, are gentler than those of metal clamps. They also deliver pressure to a broad surface and can be angled to clamp surfaces that are not parallel.

A **BAND CLAMP** is a loop of strong, woven material, such as nylon, which begins and ends at a tightening device that draws the loop smaller. Band clamps are particularly useful for clamping together shapes, such as cylinders, which don't draw together well with ordinary clamps.

SPRING CLAMPS do not exert the degree of pressure that other clamps do. They are useful for small repairs and as extra hands for holding things in place.

THE WORKING ENVIRONMENT

A good shop environment contributes to the quality and pleasure of your work. Good lighting, and plenty of it, is essen-

BUYING HAND TOOLS

Good tools contribute to good craftsmanship. Cheap tools are a waste of money—they compromise the quality of your work and the pleasure you take in it. More than once a frustrated student has thrown a poorly made chisel into the trash barrel in the first week of class.

The best tools are not necessarily the most expensive. Rosewood and brass may be seductive, but what you really want are tools that are well designed for the task at hand, durably constructed, and made to close tolerances. Fortunately, with the explosion of interest in woodworking over the past 20 years, hand tools have become readily available through retail outlets and mail-order catalogs.

tial. Fluorescent bulbs cast a generalized light that minimizes shadows and makes marking and cutting easier. Incandescent bulbs cast a warmer, more pleasant light but are far less energy efficient.

In our shop we have 3,500° Kelvin fluorescent tubes with electronic ballasts. They produce a more natural spectrum of light than cheaper fluorescents and don't have the annoying flicker and hum. We also have an area where incandescent light is available in order to see the color wood will appear in a home or gallery, which is particularly important when trying to stain wood a specific color.

A window, in addition to natural light, provides connection with the world outside. Life in the workshop joins the cycles of sun and weather. A workshop without a window can feel like a prison cell.

Order and cleanliness increase safety and efficiency. It has always been my habit to put tools away and sweep up at the end of each day's work. Not only does this allow me to find things quickly when I need them and to work without obstruction, I also feel a greater sense of excitement when I walk into a clean shop first thing in the morning.

Rare is the woodworker who feels that his or her shop is large enough. For many years I worked in one- and two-car garages. My planer was on wheels so I could roll it out of the way. When I eventually moved into a 1,200-sq.-ft. shop, I was so ecstatic that I didn't mind the absence of heat over the first winter. After several years, however, even 1,200 sq. ft. began to feel cramped.

In the long run, the size of the shop is not as important as the enjoyment you get from working in it. Wherever you work, think of your shop as a valuable tool. Take care to create a light, pleasant, orderly environment, and it will repay you handsomely.

Grinding and Sharpening

Good craftsmanship not only requires decent tools, it also demands that those tools be properly maintained. Sharp chisels and plane blades are essential. Unfortunately, many woodworkers begrudge the time sharpening takes, perhaps because they aren't very good at it. Once you have the right equipment and know how to use it, though, sharpening becomes second nature.

Two tools are used in the process of sharpening Western-style chisels: a grinding wheel and sharpening stones. The grinding wheel shapes and maintains the bevel at the business end of the blade, giving it a "hollow grind." The stones hone the leading edge of the bevel, the cutting edge, to ultimate sharpness. (Japanese chisels require flat bevels and are accordingly sharpened entirely on honing stones.) If you are just learning to grind and sharpen, it is easier to practice on a wide chisel.

Grinding

Electric grinders are usually mounted with two gray aluminum oxide wheels, one coarse and one medium. As explained on p. 52, I prefer to substitute an 80-grit, white, aluminum-oxide wheel because of its relatively soft binder and improved cutting action.

Sometimes a buffing wheel is substituted for one of the grinding wheels for the purpose of honing chisels and plane blades. This is a mistake. The tiny bevel created by a buffing wheel breaks a cardinal rule of sharpening, which is to keep the back of the blade perfectly flat. A flat back is imperative in a chisel because it is the reference surface for accurate paring. Buffing wheels are more appropriate for sharpening carving tools.

HOW TO GRIND A BEVEL The goal of grinding is to create a uniform hollow bevel across the end of the blade. The hollow is the concave surface left by the circumference of the grinding wheel. Its purpose is to save time in the honing process. With a hollow bevel in place, you spend a lot less time in the relatively slow process of honing on stones in order to affect the cutting edge (see the drawing on p. 75). A blade requires grinding when it is nicked or when its bevel becomes too flat from repeated honings.

To the unpracticed eye, a perfectly ground blade looks as though it has a straight, sharp edge. Examined under a magnifying glass, however, the edge reveals itself to be unevenly serrated by the abrasive scratches from the wheel. The ideal of a perfect edge can never be attained, but the more closely it is approximated, the sharper a blade will be. After grinding, sharpening stones are employed to create ever-more-polished, less-serrated edges.

The steps involved in grinding are as follows:

1 Adjust the grinder's tool rest. With the blade held flat on the rest, the bevel should meet the grinding wheel at the desired angle. The bevel angles of chisels and plane irons can be anywhere from 25° to 30°. To check the angle, measure the bevel with a protractor (see the photo above).

2 Turn the grinder on and hold the blade just shy of the spinning wheel. The hand position that works best for me entails holding the blade flat on the tool rest with

1

Check the bevel angle with a protractor.

2

Before you begin grinding, sight between the blade and the grinding wheel to make sure the tool rest is adjusted to the correct angle.

my thumbs and using the edges of my forefingers as guides along the lower lip of the rest.

3 With your hands in position and the blade held flat on the tool rest, slide the blade up until it makes light contact with the wheel.

4 Move the blade from side to side, keeping it flat on the tool rest and square to the face of the grinding wheel. The side-to-side movement helps to grind an even bevel and wears the wheel uniformly. (Grinding a curved blade, such as that of a scrub plane, involves moving the blade with an arcing motion.)

Grinding takes practice, but I find that, within a week, any student who is determined has mastered the art of sharpening. Fortunately, grinding is like riding a bicycle—once you have the skill, you don't lose it.

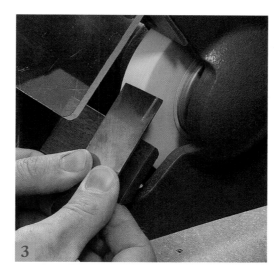

3

To grind a bevel, hold the blade flat on the tool rest with your thumbs.

4

A properly ground bevel has consistent grind marks from heel to toe.

Honing

Honing is the process of working steel on sharpening stones. After a blade has been ground to a hollow bevel, it can be honed a number of times before the hollow disappears enough to warrant regrinding.

Sharpening stones are either man-made or natural and are generally used with either oil or water as a lubricant to prevent clogging. Natural oilstones are called, in order of increasing fineness, washita, soft arkansas, hard arkansas, and black arkansas. They are lubricated with oil (we use mineral oil thinned with mineral spirits) and were the traditional choice of American craftsmen. Coarser man-made oilstones, which go by names such as crystolon and India, are often used in combination with natural stones.

Man-made, Japanese waterstones are my preference for most sharpening applications. Compared with oilstones, they have a relatively soft binder holding their abrasive particles together. On the downside, this means that they wear away more quickly and must be reflattened frequently. Their upside is that fresh abrasive particles are constantly exposed, so that they cut faster and more efficiently than oilstones. Perhaps the best aspect of waterstones is that they are lubricated with water, which eliminates oil on tools, fingers, rags, and wood.

There are two other types of sharpening stones—diamond and ceramic. Diamond stones don't leave fine enough scratch patterns to be useful in honing an edge, but they are great for keeping waterstones flat. Ceramic stones are relatively useless be-

STONE SEQUENCE

The waterstone sequence I used for years, and which our students still learn on, is to go from 1,000 grit directly to 6,000 grit. However, I find that I get even better results from a 1,000-4,000-8,000 series. The reason we don't teach students on an 8,000-grit stone is that it is extremely soft, and a beginner will repeatedly gouge the stone before getting the feel of the process.

If you prefer to work with oilstones, an equivalent sequence would be soft arkansas, white arkansas, and hard black arkansas.

cause their surfaces can't be renewed when the abrasive gets dull, which it does fairly quickly as compared with diamond.

FLATTENING THE BACK The first rule of sharpening is that the back side of the blade must stay perfectly flat. (It is all right to leave small hollows in the back of a blade, as long as they don't occur along the cutting edge.)

New chisels and plane irons always need to have their backs flattened and polished. The process can be arduous, but it is absolutely necessary. Begin by purchasing a piece of ⅜-in. seamed glass, measuring about 5 in. by 12 in. Cover one side with 100-grit psa sandpaper and the other with 220 grit. This paper is available in rolls from hardware and woodworking stores, but you can always spray-mount ordinary sandpaper instead.

Rub the back of the blade flat on the 100-grit paper until all the original factory milling marks are vanquished from the area just behind the cutting edge. (It is impossible to overstress the necessity of keeping the back FLAT on the sandpaper and stones throughout this process.) Then switch to 220 grit to remove the 100-grit scratches. Likewise, move from 220- to a 1,000-grit waterstone and from there to a 6,000-grit waterstone, so that each new abrasive removes all scratches from the previous one. Work sandpaper dry, but keep the surfaces of your waterstones wet and flat.

By the time you are finished, the back of the blade should approach a mirror finish. From then on, it should make contact

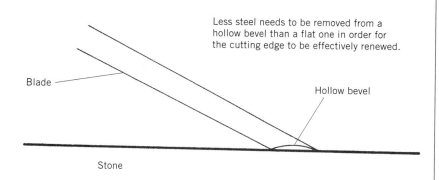

Less steel needs to be removed from a hollow bevel than a flat one in order for the cutting edge to be effectively renewed.

Blade

Hollow bevel

Stone

only with your finest sharpening stone and never need flattening again.

HONING ON STONES Whether a blade is newly ground or simply needs rehoning, the process of sharpening on stones is the same. These instructions are for a 1,000-grit/6,000-grit waterstone sequence but can be adapted for any other abrasive combination you prefer:

1 Place the bevel edge flat on the 1,000-grit waterstone. When you can feel both the toe and heel of the hollow grind in contact with the stone, lift the handle just a hair, so that only the front edge makes contact.

2 Push the blade forward with a light downward pressure. Bring the blade back with no downward pressure at all.

3 To keep the blade at a constant angle, move your body from the legs and keep your arms rigid.

4 Vary the position of each stroke in order to wear the surface of the stone evenly.

When honing on stones, keep your arms rigid and move from your legs to maintain the blade at a constant angle.

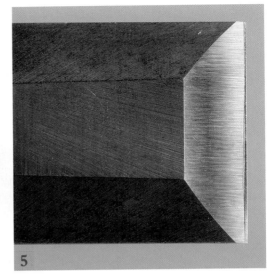

A blade only needs to be honed until the entire cutting edge is affected.

5 Hone until the cutting edge has been affected all the way across. On a freshly ground blade you can gauge this by the appearance of the steel, which will reflect light differently where it is honed (see the photo above). On subsequent sharpenings you must feel the back of the blade for the wire

edge that has been pushed over from the bevel side.

At this point, lay the back of the blade flat on the 6,000-grit stone and pull off the wire edge. The motion is just like flattening the back.

Repeat steps 1 through 5 on the 6,000-grit stone. You won't be able to feel the wire edge this time, but pretend it's there and pull it off again. A few more strokes on the bevel side, another pull-off on the back, and soon the blade should be sharp enough to shave with. When I am busy in the shop, the backs of my hands are bald from testing chisels for sharpness. A cutting edge this sharp not only makes planing, paring, and chopping a pleasure, it also is intrinsic to quality craftsmanship.

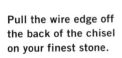

Pull the wire edge off the back of the chisel on your finest stone.

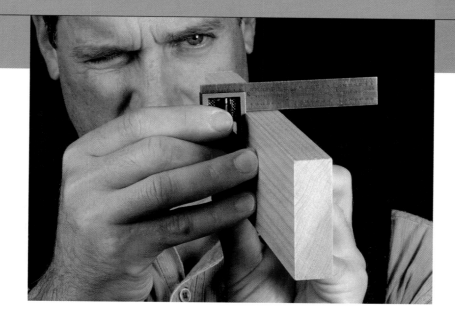

PROJECT 1

Milling a Board Four-Square

THIS CHAPTER PRESENTS the first in a series of exercises that build upon one another sequentially. If you are already competent at the machine milling process and handplaning, you might read this chapter as a review. If this information is new to you or if you are still learning, practice milling a board four-square before going on to the more complex projects that follow.

"Milling a board four-square" means cutting a piece of lumber to thickness, width, and length, and making it straight, flat, and square-edged in the process. The machines most commonly used in this operation are the jointer, the thickness planer, and the table saw. This chapter also explores the use of the bandsaw, handsaws, circular saws, and handplanes.

The project may seem simple, but it incorporates many basic understandings. These include the meaning of "square," how to measure, and the safe use of machinery. Where instructions are given to use a particular machine, please review the general safety information on p. 30, as well as the individual section on that machine in the same chapter.

How to Mill Four-Square Stock

Our goal is to end up with a piece of wood ¾ in. thick by 2½ in. wide by 24 in. long. The board you start with should be larger in each dimension. Depending on how warped, bowed, or cupped the initial board is, you can expect to lose at least ⅛ in. of thickness and ¼ in. of width in the milling process. You can use any type of hardwood for this exercise. At the school we use poplar because it is inexpensive and easy to work with.

The steps in the milling process are shown at right (note that steps 4 and 5 are often reversed).

The correct way to use a square is to hold the stock firmly against the work.

What You'll Do

1. Cut a board to approximate length.
2. Rip to approximate width.
3. Flatten one face.
4. Plane the second face parallel to the first.
5. Square one edge to a flat face.
6. Rip the board to finished width.
7. Cut one end square.
8. Cut the other end square and to length.

STEP 1 Cut to approximate length.

If you start with a long board, the first thing to do is cut off a section to approximate length, using either a handsaw or a circular saw. Begin by examining the end of the board for splits and checks. If there are any, square a pencil line across the board where the cracks end and make your first cut at that location.

TO USE A SQUARE: A framing square is good for marking out rough stock, but any square with a long enough blade will do. Hold the longer arm of the framing square parallel to and firmly against the edge of the board, as shown in the photo at left. A common mistake is to hold the square by the shorter arm on top of the board, which sometimes allows the longer arm to pull away from the edge of the board.

1

Hold the board still with your knee or foot and saw with a diagonal stroke.

TO USE A HANDSAW: Make sure the board is well supported, preferably on low saw-horses to make it easier to put your weight behind the saw. Get a foot or knee on the board so it won't move. Use a crosscut saw with a diagonal, downward sawing motion, starting at the far edge of the board. Begin sawing with a pull stroke to establish the location of the cut, guiding the saw against your thumb.

TO USE A CIRCULAR SAW: Set the depth of the blade so that it extends about ¼ in. to ½ in. deeper than the thickness of the wood. Hold the board firmly in place, using either your knee, your foot, or clamps. Keep both hands on the saw for maximum control. Don't let the blade contact the wood until after you start the saw. Place the saw so the larger side of the base rests on the part of the board that will remain in place, not the offcut. Depress the trigger and push forward at a measured, steady pace. Keep the saw moving forward and hold it firmly on the board. The saw is most likely to kick if you hesitate and pull back, as you might in trying to correct the direction of the cut.

When the end of the board is free of splits, measure out 25 in. in length and square a line across.

TO MEASURE: This first measurement is only a rough one, where ¹⁄₁₆ in. or so won't matter. If you are using a tape measure, place the hook over the end of the board and pull the tape out from there. If you are using a folding rule, hold the end of the unfolded rule even with the end of the board. For measurements where greater accuracy is required, measure from the 1-in. mark on the tape or rule (see the photo below).

1

Measure from the 1-in. mark for measurements where greater accuracy is required. Remember to add the extra inch to your measurement.

Make sure you measure to a number 1 in. greater than the one you actually want. Once in a while I forget to add the extra inch and come up with a piece of wood an inch too short.

Cut the board to length, again using a handsaw or circular saw.

STEP 2 Rip to approximate width.

Next, rip the board to approximate width, using a handsaw, bandsaw, or table saw. Leave at least ¼ in. extra width over the 2½ in. we are aiming for. I prefer to rip with a bandsaw, which is safer than a table saw and easier than a handsaw.

TO RIP WITH A BANDSAW: Rather than put a fence on the bandsaw, which requires setting the drift (see pp.40–41), I mark the

width directly on the board with a pencil and straightedge, and bandsaw freehand.

For safety, set the blade guard just above the thickness of the wood. Always push forward as you saw—if you pull the board back in the middle of a bandsaw cut, you can pull the blade off the wheels.

TO RIP ON A TABLE SAW: Ripping rough lumber to width on a table saw is common practice but is more dangerous than using a bandsaw. A board that is warped or has curved edges (as rough lumber often does) has a greater chance of binding against the blade and kicking back. If you are ripping with a table saw, you should first look to see if the edge that will run against the rip fence is straight. If not, straighten it on a jointer before proceeding (see pp. 83–84).

Use a square to verify that the sawblade is set square to the table.

2

Set the rip fence to the desired distance from the sawblade.

TOOL TIP

If the board is cupped, put the convex side face down against the table when ripping on the table saw. If the concave side were down, the elevated center of the board would drop to the table at the completion of the cut, possibly binding between the blade and the fence. If the board is badly cupped, hold the section between the blade and the fence as flat as possible against the table. ■

Install a rip or combination blade and make sure it is set square to the table. If you have any doubt after checking the blade with a square, make a sample cut on a scrap board.

■ Set the rip fence to the desired width, about 2¾ in. away from the blade in this case. To double-check the setting of your rip fence, measure the distance from the fence to a saw tooth that hooks toward it (see the photo above).

■ Raise the blade a tooth's height over the thickest part of the wood to be sawn.

■ Have a push stick handy to complete the cut.

■ Turn the saw on and feed the board through as steadily as possible. Keep the edge of the board against the fence at all times. To avoid binding and kickback, do not let go of the board under any circumstance until the cut is com-

2

Set the sawblade a tooth's height above the wood.

plete and the board has entirely passed the sawblade.

■ Do not let your left hand go any further forward than the near end of the throat plate. A common mistake is to hold wood against the fence with your left hand next to or beyond the blade, which puts your hand in position to be drawn into the blade should a kickback occur.

RIPPING ON THE TABLE SAW

BEFORE RIPPING, it is imperative that your table saw be set up safely, as described on pp. 36–38. If the fence is parallel to the blade and you have properly installed splitter, it will be a much safer and more accurate operation.

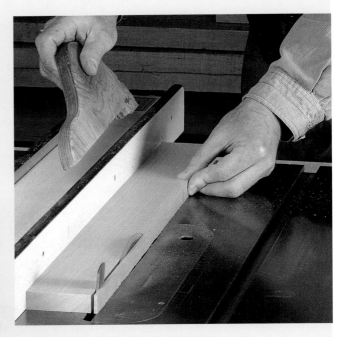

1 Start the rip cut by pushing the wood forward with your right hand while holding the board down on the saw table and firmly against the fence with your left hand.

2 Continue holding the board in position with your left hand while reaching for a push stick with your right hand.

3 Complete the cut by releasing your left hand and following through with the push stick until the board is completely beyond the sawblade.

- Use the push stick to complete the cut, rather than passing your right hand near the blade. The push stick should be centered on the section of wood that will pass between the blade and the fence. If the push stick is too close to the fence, it can steer the front end of the board away from the fence, somewhat like the rudder of a boat.

- For safety, do not get in the habit of reaching for the offcut while the blade is still running. Don't worry, it can't kick back violently, even though the blade may push it toward you. To remove the offcut, either turn the saw off and wait for the blade to be still or push it away with another piece of wood so your hand stays clear of the blade.

TO RIP WITH A HANDSAW:

- Mark the desired width on the board with a pencil and straightedge.

- Be sure that you are using a ripsaw. A crosscut saw is ineffectual for ripping.

- Support the board across two sawhorses.

- Saw up to, but not through, the line. Try to keep the sawn edge square to the face of the board.

STEP 3 Flatten one face.

Once the board has been cut to approximate length and width, the next step is to flatten one face with a jointer or handplanes.

If you are using a jointer, be sure the knives are sharp and properly set. If not, refer to the machine's manual. The jointer's fence should be located at the far edge of the table, allowing access to virtually the full width of the knives. Only when the knives have been nicked or dulled at the far end, where they receive the most use, does the fence need to be moved to a narrower position.

TO USE A JOINTER:

- Set the infeed table to take off no more than 1⁄16 in. per pass. If necessary, you can gauge the depth of cut with a straightedge placed flat on the outfeed table and extending over the infeed table (see the photo below). Assuming the outfeed table is correctly set, tangent to the apex of the knives, the height of the straightedge off the infeed table equals the depth of cut. Usually, I gauge the depth of cut by the feel of the first pass.

Gauge the depth of cut on a jointer by placing a straightedge flat on the outfeed table and extending it over the infeed table.

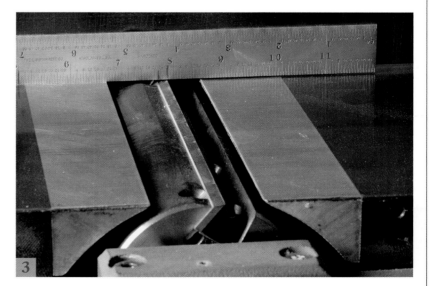

- Determine which face of the board you will joint. I prefer to flatten the more concave face because it sits more steadily on the table.

- Decide in which direction the board should be fed in order to cut with the grain as much as possible (see p. 7 and the drawing on p. 42).

- Turn the machine on, place the board face down on the infeed table, and push the board through at a steady pace with its edge against the fence. At the start of the cut, hold the board down on the infeed table. When about half of the board has passed the cutterhead, shift your downward weight to the outfeed table. Don't push down too hard, though. If you force a warped board flat against the jointer table, it will just spring back to its natural shape at the end of the pass.

- Don't release the board before the cut is complete.

- Take as many passes as necessary to remove all dips and hollows.

- When the newly jointed face is completely smooth and flat, you may want to pencil on a check mark for later reference.

TOOL TIP

When using a jointer, work with a push stick in your right hand and a hold-down in your left. You may not always be able to use these when working with longer boards, but do so whenever you can. ■

TO USE HANDPLANES:

The tools used to flatten the face of a board by hand are a flat workbench, a scrub plane, and a bench plane. For this project I used a 14-in. jack plane, but longer planes work just as well or better. The scrub plane is for quick wood removal during the initial stage of flattening wide and cupped boards. It can be dispensed with when planing a reasonably flat, small board.

Handplaning may seem daunting at first, but it quickly becomes a pleasure. The secret is to have a well-tuned plane with a razor-sharp blade. Resharpen blades often (see pp. 72–76 for a discussion of grinding and sharpening). When planing, lift the plane off the wood on the return stroke to keep the blade sharp longer. When a plane is not in use, rest it on its side, rather than its sole, for the same reason.

The ways in which a board might not be flat are characterized as cup, twist, and bow (see pp. 8–9). While there is more than one way to plane a board flat, the procedure I suggest is to remove the cup first, the twist second, and the bow third.

- Choose which side of the board to flatten. I find it easier to flatten the more convex side first.

- Clamp the board flat on top of the workbench, preferably with bench dogs and a tail vise. If the board rocks, place small wedges underneath to steady it.

- If there is noticeable cup to the board, remove it with a scrub plane. (If necessary, substitute any bench plane.) Set the blade of your scrub plane to extend about ¹⁄₁₆ in. beyond the sole. To avoid

FLATTENING THE FIRST FACE ON A JOINTER

G IVEN THE CHOICE between flattening lumber with a jointer or a handplane, woodworkers generally choose the jointer for convenience and speed. While there is a romance to handplaning that a jointer can't touch, it's also true that working skillfully and efficiently with machinery becomes a pleasing dance in and of itself.

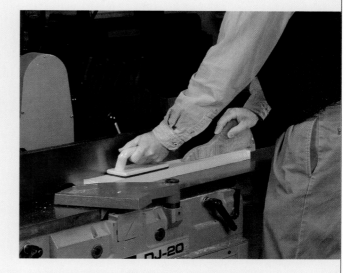

1 Hold the board down on the infeed table and against the fence with a hold-down while pushing it over the cutterhead with a push stick.

2 As the board passes over the cutterhead, transfer your weight to hold the board against the outfeed table.

3 Follow through with the push stick in your right hand until the board is completely beyond the cutterhead and the cutterhead guard swings shut.

Plane across the grain with a scrub plane to begin flattening a board with significant cup.

Use winding sticks to check the board for twist.

tearout, plane across the grain. Cover the entire surface of the board with parallel strokes. Avoid planing material off the very edges of the board, because they are already the lowest spots. Plane until the cup has been removed. You will have a rough surface at this point.

■ Use a pair of winding sticks (straight sticks of uniform width) to determine the degree of twist. Place a stick across each end of the board and sight across their tops to reveal the amount of twist.

■ Remove the twist by planing the ends of the board to bring them into alignment. Work with your bench plane. It doesn't matter whether you plane across the grain, on the diagonal, or with the grain. What you are trying to do is keep the board flat across while taking down the high corners at one or both ends, until the winding sticks read parallel.

■ Now check the length of the board for bow with a straightedge. Most likely the board is high at the center, particularly if you have planed the ends to remove twist. In this case, take long strokes from end to end with your bench plane, but start the cut with the blade already on the wood and lift it off just before reaching the far end. This takes out the bow without dropping the ends. As you plane, the valleys and ridges left by the curved blade of the scrub plane disappear and you begin to get long shavings. The depth of cut should be slight, yielding thin, limp shavings without much resistance. When the board becomes flat or slightly concave along its length, take strokes all the way through both ends.

■ At this point the board is a whole lot flatter than when you started, but some cup or twist may have crept back in. Repeat the entire process of checking for and removing cup, twist, and bow, but this time use a newly sharpened bench plane throughout, taking light shavings. When the board is flat you will be able to take perfect, continuous shavings from one end to the other.

■ Mark the newly jointed face with a pencil for later reference.

STEP 4 Plane the second face parallel to the first.

If we were to flatten the second face on a jointer, as we did the first, we would have two flat sides that bore no particular relationship to each other. A jointer flattens a surface only in reference to itself; it doesn't know anything about the other side of the board. We want to make the second face parallel to the first, in which case it will automatically be just as flat. This can be done with a thickness planer or with handplanes.

TO USE A THICKNESS PLANER:

■ Check that the knives are sharp and properly set. If they are not, refer to the machine's manual.

■ Establish the correct depth of cut. With the machine turned off, adjust the opening between table and cutterhead so that it is wide enough for the board to pass through freely. Then raise the table or lower the cutterhead (whichever your machine does) until the thickest part of the board is pinched under the infeed roller. Increase the opening just enough to remove the board, remove it, and reclose the gap.

■ Decide which end of the board should be fed in first to cut with the grain as much as possible (see p. 7 and the drawing on p. 44).

Take out twist and bow with a bench plane.

Feed the board through the thickness planer to achieve the desired thickness.

■ Turn the machine on and feed the board in. Remember, the previously flattened side goes face down against the table; the rough side goes up to meet the cutterhead. The infeed roller will grab the board and pull it through. All you need to do is keep the board straight and catch it as it comes out the back.

Scribe the desired thickness around the edges of the board before handplaning the second face.

4

■ Once you've made the first pass, reduce the distance between the cutterhead and the table by ¹⁄₁₆ in. (or less) and take another pass. Depending on your planer, either a full turn or a half turn of the crank should be about ¹⁄₁₆ in.

■ When the entire second surface has been affected by the action of the planer, start flipping the board end-for-end with each pass. The idea is to take approximately the same amount of wood off of both faces to keep their moisture content balanced.

■ Stop planing when the board measures the intended thickness.

TO USE HANDPLANES:

■ Scribe the desired thickness around all four edges of the board with a marking gauge or a cutting gauge.

■ Clamp the board on the surface of the workbench between bench dogs.

■ Plane off most of the excess with a scrub plane. To avoid tearout, plane across the grain.

■ Plane down to the scribed line with a bench plane, working with the grain.

STEP **5** Square one edge to the flat face.

Now that both faces of the board are flat, either can be used as a reference for making one edge straight and square with a jointer or handplane.

TO SQUARE AN EDGE WITH A JOINTER:

■ Set the jointer fence square to the table. Check the angle of the fence with a square placed on the outfeed table just behind the cutterhead. To be sure the fence is properly set, make a test pass on a piece of scrap, and check it for squareness.

■ Check the depth of cut. The jointer should remove no more than ¹⁄₁₆ in. at a pass. Thicker settings are more likely to cause tearout where the grain changes direction.

■ Turn the machine on and run the board through, cutting with the grain as much as possible. Hold the flat face firmly against the fence and the board edge down on the table. Shift your weight from infeed to outfeed as the first foot of the board passes on to the cutterhead.

- Use a push stick in your right hand. With your left hand, hold the board against the fence and down on the table (see photo at right). With wider boards you can safely pass your left hand above the blade guard. With a narrow board such as the one in this exercise it is more prudent to stop your left hand before it reaches the blade guard and then, when enough of the board has crossed over, reach over the blade guard to hold the wood against the outfeed table and the fence.

- Take repeated passes until the edge of the board is uniformly milled.

- Mark the newly jointed edge with a check mark for later reference.

Square an edge to a previously flattened face on the jointer.

SHOOTING BOARD FOR HANDPLANING

Squaring an edge freehand with a handplane is diffi-cult, so traditional woodworkers came up with a simple device to aid in this process. This is the shooting board (see the drawing at right). It consists of a flat board screwed onto a wider flat board, sometimes with a stop at one end of the top board. This is an excellent use for MDF, but smooth plywood or real lumber work too. All the shooting board is expected to do is keep your handplane at a constant angle to the work.

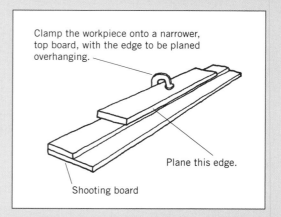

Clamp the workpiece onto a narrower, top board, with the edge to be planed overhanging.

Plane this edge.

Shooting board

TO SQUARE AN EDGE WITH A HANDPLANE:

- Clamp the work on the shooting board, flat face down. The edge to be planed should protrude a little beyond the edge of the narrower top board and be fairly parallel with it.

- Set the iron of your longest bench plane to cut parallel with the sole. (A 22-in. jointer plane is ideal.)

- Begin planing the edge of the board. With the plane resting on its side, take long through strokes against the protruding edge. Hold the side of the plane firmly down on the shooting board to keep the angle constant.

When working on a shooting board, use your longest bench plane and keep it flat on its side at all times.

- Stop for a moment to check the newly planed edge for squareness to the flat face. If it is off, adjust the angle of the plane iron accordingly and begin again.

- When the entire edge has been planed, take a series of strokes that don't quite reach either end. When the blade ceases to cut, the edge will be slightly concave. Then take one or two full shavings all the way through and, voilà, you have a straight, flat, square edge.

- Mark the square edge with a pencil for future reference.

STEP 6 Rip the board to finished width.

One edge of the board remains to be cut to width, flattened, and squared. I use a table saw for this step, but you could choose a handsaw or bandsaw and finish up with a bench plane.

To use a table saw, refer to the directions on pp. 80–83. Otherwise, mark the desired width on the board with a pencil and straightedge. If there is enough excess, cut carefully to (but not through) the line with a bandsaw or ripsaw. After you saw (or if there was not enough excess to saw), plane to the line, straight and square, with the longest benchplane you have. Work freehand or with a shooting board. Remember to check the edge for squareness to the face as you go along.

STEP 7 Cut one end square.

Our board now measures ¾ in. by 2½ in. and has four flat, straight sides that are square to one another. The next step is to

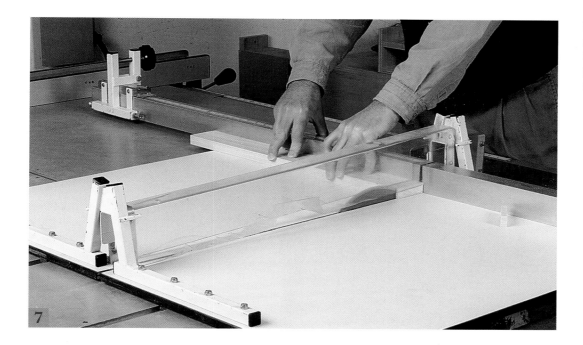

cut one end square with a table saw, a chopsaw, or a backsaw.

TO USE A TABLE SAW:

For crosscutting on a table saw, it is necessary to use a miter gauge or a sliding table. The rip fence should be well out of the way.

▪ Set the blade square to the table and a tooth's height above the thickness of the wood.

▪ If you are using a miter gauge, check it for square. A sliding table should always be square. If it is not square, either fix it or replace it. There is no use cluttering up the shop with inaccurate equipment.

▪ Turn the machine on and make the cut. The board should be held firmly against the fence of the miter gauge or sliding table. You only need remove enough length to square the end. Make sure your fingers are not in the line of the

cut. Remember, the blade will come through the back of the miter gauge or sliding table as you complete the cut.

▪ Safely retrieve the workpiece. Once the cut has been made, pull the wood back to the starting position in one continuous motion, keeping it firmly against the fence of the miter gauge or sliding table the whole time. Don't stop with the wood in contact with the sawblade. Turn the machine off and let the blade stop spinning before you lift the board off the saw or reach for the offcut.

▪ Check the end for squareness.

TO USE A CHOPSAW:

If you are using a chopsaw, you might want to check it for squareness by cutting a test piece first. Hold the wood firmly against the fence and make sure that you keep your fingers out of the path of the blade.

7

The second saw cut uses the kerf from the first saw cut as a guide down the face of the board.

TO USE A BACKSAW:

There are two approaches to marking for a backsaw cut. For a less rigorous square end, like this one, it is fine to saw to a pencil line. For greater precision, as when sawing the shoulders of a joint, saw to a knife line. In either case, cutting a square end by hand takes practice.

■ Carefully square a line around one end of the board with a sharp pencil. Leave at least 3⁄16 in. of waste on the outside of the line to help hold the saw in its kerf. Good work depends on good marking. The pencil lines should be fine and meet exactly at each corner.

■ Clamp the wood firmly in a vise or over the edge of a benchtop.

■ Hold the saw at a diagonal on the near corner. Begin with a backstroke to establish the kerf, steadying the saw against your thumb. Saw down and across at the same time. Sawing on the face and edge simultaneously keeps the cut square in both dimensions. I find I do my most accurate sawing if I saw just off the line. Leaving a miniscule bit of wood between a saw cut and a pencil line makes it easier to see that you are sawing parallel to the line.

■ Once the full diagonal is sawn, turn the board 90° toward you and make a new diagonal cut. The previous kerf will guide the saw down the face of the board.

■ When the second diagonal is complete, turn the board another 90° to saw the last face. Once again, saw a diagonal.

■ Place the saw straight across the kerf you just made and saw straight down till the end of the board falls off. The kerfs on either side will guide the saw if you let them.

STEP **8** Cut the other end square and to length.

The final step is to cut the second end square and to length. Measure out 24 in. from the square end. Use a square and pencil to mark the length around all four sides. Cut as you did in step 7.

PROJECT 2

Cutting a Mortise and Tenon

THE MORTISE AND TENON is the most important joint in furniture making. There is no stronger or more permanent means of joining two pieces of wood together in situations where the end of one board meets the edge of another. Mortise-and-tenon joints can be cut with hand tools, power tools, or various combinations of the two.

Simple mortise-and-tenon joints that meet at right angles can be made satisfactorily with power tools, but the ability to cut a mortise and tenon by hand opens up a much wider range of applications and design possibilities. In this chapter, we will go through the step-by-step process of cutting a simple, blind mortise and tenon by hand.

The skills involved—measuring, marking, sawing, chopping and paring with chisels, sharpening, and fitting—are basic building blocks of wood craftsmanship.

Don't expect your first, second, or third mortise and tenon to be perfect. The first one may be terrible, but each subsequent one will be an improvement. Once you master the process, you will be technically and psychologically ready to learn any aspect of furniture making.

To prepare for this project, cut the piece of wood milled in the previous project in half to make two pieces ¾ in. by 2½ in. by approximately 12 in. long. The exact lengths aren't important, but make sure the ends are square.

The experience of cutting a mortise and tenon is affected by the species of wood. A soft hardwood, such as poplar, cuts and assembles relatively easily; the wood compresses enough to forgive some fatness in the joint. A denser wood such as cherry offers greater resistance to the saw and chisel and must be cut to closer tolerances for a good fit, but it also works much cleaner and crisper.

Cutting a Mortise

Mortises are almost always cut before tenons because there is more flexibility in sizing a tenon to fit a mortise than the other way around. The general rule for thickness, when joining a frame, is that a mortise should be approximately one-third as thick as the wood into which it is cut. The specific thickness of a hand-cut mortise is determined by the nearest size of chisel. For example, a mortise cut in a piece of ¾-in. wood should be ¼ in. thick, with ¼-in. shoulders on each side. A mortise cut in a piece of ⅞-in. wood could be either ¼ in. or ⁵⁄₁₆ in. thick, as long as you have both size chisels to choose from.

The depth of a mortise should be at least twice, and preferably three times, its

MORTISE-AND-TENON PROPORTIONS

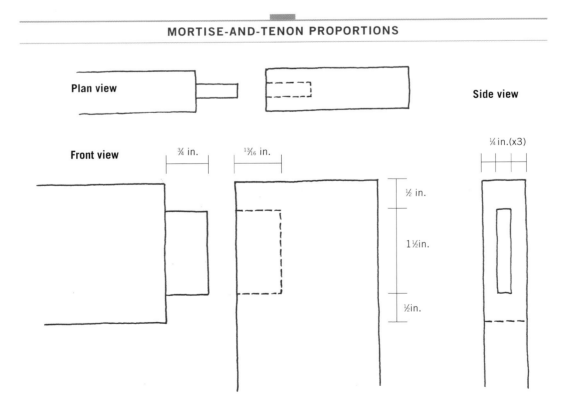

Plan view

Side view

Front view

¾ in.

¹³⁄₁₆ in.

¼ in.(x3)

½ in.

1½in.

½in.

What You'll Need

- ☐ Folding rule
- ☐ Mortise gauge
- ☐ Marking knife
- ☐ Square
- ☐ Mallet
- ☐ ¼-in. and 1-in. chisels
- ☐ Drill with a ³⁄₁₆-in. or ¼-in. brad-point bit
- ☐ Pencil

thickness. It also should be a little deeper than the anticipated length of the tenon, just to be sure the tenon won't bottom out. The width can vary considerably. Our mortise will be ¼ in. thick, ¹³⁄₁₆ in. deep, and 1½ in. wide, with ½-in. shoulders at each end (see the drawing on the facing page).

There are many ways to cut a mortise. The most basic is to chop it out with a mortise chisel and a mallet. At the other end of the spectrum are mortises machined with horizontal slot mortisers or hollow-chisel mortisers. Mortises can also be

What You'll Do

1. Mark out the mortise.
2. Pare back to the knife line from within the mortise.
3. Drill out the waste.
4. Chop down just shy of the ends.
5. Pare down the sides and remove the waste.
6. Chop the ends to the knife line.
7. Pare the sides square and the bottom clean.

Butt both pieces together and mark their faces for reference.

made with routers, as we shall see on pp. 166–167. The method presented here emphasizes hand skills but employs a drill press for quick removal of waste. It is reasonably efficient and offers substantial control, leading to accurate results with practice.

STEP 1 Mark out the mortise.

First, decide which of the two pieces of ¾-in. by 2½-in. by 12-in. wood is for the mortise and which is for the tenon. Position them with the tenon piece butting against the mortise piece to form a corner. Mark the face of each board so you'll remember how they go together (see the photo above). Later, when you use the mortise gauge, be sure to mark from the "face" side of each board. Scribing from the face of one and the back of the other would misalign the joint to the extent that the gauge wasn't perfectly centered.

To mark the mortise width, measure in ½ in. and 2 in. from the end of the board on the edge where the mortise will be located. Mark each measurement with a knife prick. Square the marks across the wood with a knife.

Mark the mortise ends square across the edge of the board with a knife.

Scribe the mortise thickness with a mortise gauge.

To mark the mortise thickness, set the mortise gauge so that the distance between the pins is just over ¼ in. The extra smidge helps ensure that the chisel won't stick in the mortise. Then set the distance from the fence to the nearest pin at ¼ in. With the shoulder of the gauge firmly against the face of the board, scribe the thickness of the mortise from knife line to knife line, as shown in the bottom photo at left. I find it easiest to pull the gauge with the pins angled slightly away so they drag rather than dig in.

For this project, there is no reason to have a perfectly centered mortise, but if you want one, set the gauge as explained above. Then use it to make pin pricks from opposite faces of the board in the same location. If they coincide, the gauge is centered. If not, readjust the fence until they match.

Save the setting on the mortise gauge for marking the tenon.

STEP 2 **Pare back to the knife line.**

Hold the wood between bench dogs, in a vise or clamped to the benchtop. Working from the waste side, pare back to the knife lines at each end of the mortise with a sharp ¼-in. chisel. Pare with the bevel down for greater control. Paring creates a straight-backed groove that will guide the chisel while chopping the ends in step 6 (see p. 100).

Although it's good practice to pare back to marks cut across the grain with a knife, as we are doing here, don't pare back to the indents you made with the pins of the mortise gauge. They are ideal just as they are for starting a chisel cut

PARING BACK TO THE KNIFE LINE

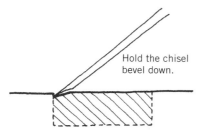

Hold the chisel bevel down.

Paring back to the knife line creates a straight-backed groove that will guide the chisel in chopping the mortise ends.

TOOL TIP

Whenever you pare with a chisel, keep both hands behind the blade. More than once I have seen students ignore this advice and stab themselves. A bench dog, stop, or vise should be used to hold the board steady, not a hand in front of the blade. ■

with the grain, where there is far less resistance.

STEP 3 Drill out the waste.

Drill out the waste with a ¼-in. or smaller brad-point bit. Begin with holes about ⅛ in. from each end, then connect them with a series of (ideally) contiguous holes. The small amount of wood left at each end gives you something to pry against when chiseling out waste without denting the finished lip of the mortise.

Use a drill press, electric drill, or hand drill. If you are using a drill press, the edge of the board that sits on the table must be square to the sides; otherwise the holes will run crooked. The extension slide on a folding rule is useful for checking the depth of the first hole.

Don't worry if you happen to drill a little bit beyond the scribe lines for the cheeks. The joint will still come out fine. The half-moon indentation that remains in the cheek after you've cleaned out the waste will reveal whether you've pared straight or crooked by the uniformity of its width from top to bottom.

Use a chisel to pare back to the knife lines at each end of the mortise.

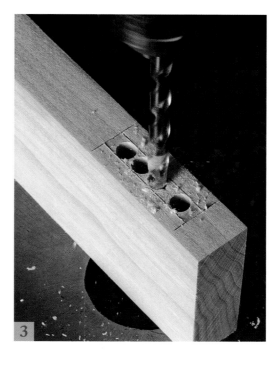

Drill out the mortise waste with a series of near-contiguous holes, using a drill press, electric drill, or hand drill.

TO USE A DRILL PRESS:

- Make sure the table is set square to the bit. Adjust the height of the table to bring the wood close to the bit.

- Set the depth stop to make holes that will go $^{13}/_{16}$ in. beyond the surface of the wood.

- When drilling a piece this size, hold the wood firmly on the drill table with your free hand. Smaller pieces, which might spin out of control, should be clamped in place or held against a fixed fence.

- Although I usually eyeball the locations of the holes as I drill, you may prefer to clamp a fence on the drill table as a guide. The holes don't have to be perfectly centered within the mortise.

TO USE AN ELECTRIC DRILL OR HAND DRILL:

- Wrap masking tape around the drill bit, $^{13}/_{16}$ in. from the cutting edge, to indicate the desired depth.

- Clamp the wood firmly in a vise or to your bench.

- Visually align the drill from the front and the side to make sure you are drilling as straight as possible.

- If desired, scribe a line down the center of the mortise with a marking gauge to provide a pilot location for the bit.

STEP 4 Chop down just shy of the ends.

Hold the wood on the benchtop with bench dogs or a clamp. Locate your ¼-in. chisel at the edges of the holes closest to the ends (see the photo at bottom left) with the bevel facing inward. Drive the chisel with a mallet until it hits the bottom

Chop clear to the bottom where the holes have been drilled at both ends.

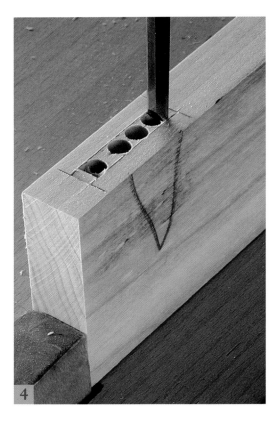

Pare down the sides of the mortise with a 1-in. chisel.

PARING DOWN THE SIDES

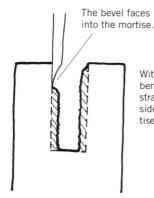

The bevel faces into the mortise.

With a wide bench chisel, cut straight down the sides of the mortise.

6

Chop the ends of the mortise to the knife line.

of the mortise. You can do this without much resistance because the holes provide space into which the waste can collapse.

Although this mortise will be invisible once the joint is assembled, the goal is to have crisp, clean corners and edges. Good work is good work, whether or not it will be seen.

STEP 5 Pare down the sides.

Set your 1-in. chisel in one of the small grooves left by the mortise gauge. The bevel should face into the mortise. Position yourself so you are looking down the length of the board, which enables

you to see if the chisel is vertical. Gently tap the chisel with a mallet to cut straight down the side of the mortise. Don't drive the chisel too far, or the wood will split. The chisel should be razor sharp (for instructions on sharpening chisels, see pp. 72–76).

When you have cut partway down both sides in this fashion, use the ¼-in. chisel to clean out the waste. Resume paring the sides, cleaning out the waste as you go, until you reach the bottom of the mortise.

CHOPPING TO A KNIFE LINE

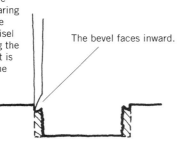

The straight-backed groove created by paring to a knife line keeps the chisel from crossing the shoulder as it is driven into the wood.

The bevel faces inward.

PRYING OUT THE CORNERS

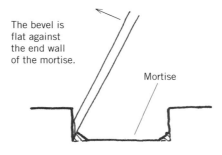

The bevel is flat against the end wall of the mortise.

Mortise

STEP **6** Chop the ends back to the knife line.

Rest the ¼-in. chisel against the knife line at each end of the mortise. The bevel should face inward (see the bottom left drawing on p. 99). The small shoulder that you created by paring back to the line in step 2 prevents the chisel from pushing beyond the knife line as you force it into the wood.

Drive the chisel straight down with a mallet, chopping clear to the bottom of the mortise. To clean out the bottom cor-

ners at each end, tap the chisel in with the bevel flat against the end wall of the mortise (see the bottom right drawing on p. 99). By prying with the bevel against the wall of the mortise, you can avoid denting the lip of the mortise.

STEP **7** Pare the cheeks and ends square and the bottom clean.

The cheeks of the mortise should be square to the surface. Check this by holding the back of a chisel flat against each cheek, as shown in the photo below, and sliding a small square up to it. If a cheek is angled into the mortise, gradually pare it square. If a cheek is angled such that the mortise gets wider at the bottom, just live with it for now. You'll improve with practice.

Remove all waste to give the mortise a flat, clean bottom. Check the depth with a folding rule.

CUTTING A TENON

A tenon should fit a mortise snugly, like a hand in a glove. They should go together with noticeable friction, but not require

Check the mortise sides for squareness with a square and a chisel.

What You'll Need

☐ Folding rule
☐ Mortise gauge
☐ Knife
☐ Square
☐ Backsaw
☐ 1-in. and ½-in. chisels
☐ Pencil

What You'll Do

1. Measure tenon length and mark the shoulders.
2. Scribe the thickness with a mortise gauge.
3. Mark the width.
4. Pare back to the shoulders.
5. Saw the shoulders.
6. Saw the cheeks.
7. Re-mark and saw the width.
8. Clean up and fit.

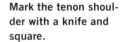

Mark the tenon shoulder with a knife and square.

pounding. An overly tight tenon can make assembly a nightmare and even split a mortise along the grain.

There is more than one right way to cut a tenon. The steps outlined above work well for me.

STEP **1** Measure tenon length and mark the shoulders.

The mortise is ¹³⁄₁₆ in. deep, and we've designed the tenon to be ¾ in. long to ensure that it doesn't hit bottom before the shoulders pull tight. With a sharp knife, mark the shoulder ¾ in. from the end of the tenon piece, and square the mark around all four sides.

Accuracy is extremely important when marking shoulders. Hold the fence of the square firmly against the wood, and hold the knife blade at a constant angle throughout each cut. Position the knife for the second cut by registering its tip in the first cut, and so on. The last cut should meet the first cut perfectly.

Register the knife tip in the first cut and slide the square into position against it to accurately mark the second shoulder.

TOOL TIP

For greatest accuracy in squaring a line around a board, always register the fence of the square against a consistent edge and a consistent face. That way, if the edges and faces weren't milled perfectly parallel, the line will still come out right. ■

Scribe the tenon thickness around the end and edges with the mortise gauge.

STEP 2 Scribe the tenon thickness.

The mortise gauge should still have the same setting that was used for the mortise. Clamp the wood upright in a vise so both of your hands are free. Place the fence of the gauge firmly against the face of the wood. Scribe the tenon thickness around the edges and end of the board, from shoulder to shoulder.

STEP 3 Mark the width.

The width of a blind tenon does not need to be cut as perfectly as its thickness. The significant glue bond will be formed between the cheeks of the tenon and the cheeks of the mortise, where long grain meets long grain. The width serves primarily to register the tenon in place.

Tenon width can be marked with a marking gauge or a pencil and square. To use the latter, which is my preference, measure in ½ in. from each side and square the width around the cheeks and end of the tenon.

Mark the width of the tenon with a pencil and square.

STEP 4 Pare back to the shoulders.

Now that the tenon is completely marked out, the next step is to pare back to the shoulders with your 1-in. chisel. We do this for the same reason we pared back to the ends of the mortise, which is to give the chisel a clean start on the final finish cut.

Lay the wood flat on the workbench. Place a bench dog or stop at the far end to keep the wood from sliding away from you. On all four sides, pare a small groove back to the knifed shoulder line from the

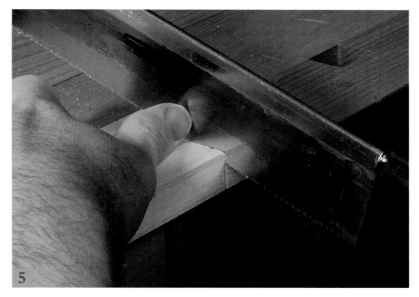

Guide the saw against your thumb as you begin
sawing diagonally on the near corner.

4

Pare back to the knife line on all four sides of
the board.

tenon side. Pare with the bevel down for
greater control. Keep both hands behind
the blade for safety.

STEP 5 Saw the shoulders.

Hold the wood in a vise or clamp it over
the edge of your benchtop. Start sawing
on a diagonal at the corner nearest you.
Begin by guiding the saw against your
thumb and starting with a couple of pull
strokes. The saw teeth should be as close
to the knife line as you can comfortably
saw without actually impinging upon it. I
usually leave about ⅟₃₂ in. Watch the saw
cut down and across at the same time.
Working in two dimensions keeps the saw
straight in both.

Saw all the way across the board and
down to the nearest scribe mark, which
denotes the location of the edge of the

Saw across the board and down to the nearest
scribe mark.

tenon. Don't saw the side of the board you
can't see.

Rotate the board 90° toward you and
saw on the diagonal once again. This time,
there will be a kerf as a vertical guide.
Stop sawing when you have cut all the

way across on the horizontal and down to the nearest scribe line. Rotate the board and repeat the diagonal sawing process two more times.

Finally, cut each shoulder down to the level of the tenon with the saw held horizontally. The existing kerfs will guide the saw.

Saw the tenon cheeks on the diagonal right to the line.

Chop back to the shoulder line in small increments.

STEP 6 Saw the cheeks.

Place the wood in a vise on an upright diagonal leaning away from you. Saw on the waste sides of the tenon up to but not through the scribe marks left by the mortise gauge. The goal is to have the tenon fit right off the saw, with minimal paring. You can saw this boldly because the cheeks will be hidden: Accidental oversawing won't create a cosmetic problem. Saw down and across simultaneously for greater control. Stop when you have cut across the end and down to the shoulder. Don't saw on the side you can't see.

Turn the board around and place it upright in the vise. Cut down the second side with the saw straight across. The existing kerf will guide the saw, if you let it. When you reach the shoulder, the waste piece should fall off the cheek. If not, the shoulder wasn't sawn deep enough in the previous step.

STEP 7 Re-mark and saw the width.

When the cheek waste falls off, the width marks go with it. Re-mark the width, then saw to the lines.

STEP 8 Clean up and fit.

Once a tenon is sawn, a certain amount of cleanup is necessary. Start with the shoulders. Hold the work flat on the bench with dogs or a clamp. Use your 1-in. chisel to chop back to the shoulders in small increments of about 1/16 in. Then turn the work on edge and use your 1/2-in. chisel on the narrow-end shoulders the same way.

TOOL TIP

An alternative way to flatten the shoulders is to use a shoulder plane, referencing the body of the plane against the cheeks of the tenon to keep the shoulders square. ■

When you're done, a straightedge should rest across the shoulders at any location without rocking. Slight back-cutting is permissible, so long as it is confined to interior sections of the shoulder, which will be invisible after assembly.

Next, try to fit the tenon into the mortise. If it is too thick or too wide, pare it down methodically to maintain squareness. Again, remember to clamp the wood or hold it in a vise while paring. Keep the back of the chisel flat against the wood to tell you where the high spots are. Pare with or across the grain, where possible, rather than against it.

The assembled joint should have a firm fit with snug shoulders. If the shoulders are not snug, either the tenon is too long or the shoulders are not flat. If the shoulders are snug on one side only, they may not be square across, or the mortise or the tenon may be crooked and require further paring.

If you feel there is room for improvement, begin again. Cut off the tenon to make the end square. Mark a mortise in a new location. Sharpen your chisels. Work carefully. Each step builds on the accuracy of previous ones.

With a reasonable commitment to practice you will master the skill of cutting a mortise and tenon with hand tools. Once you can do that, you can do anything!

The component parts of the mortise and tenon.

The completed mortise and tenon should draw tight at the shoulders.

PROJECT 3

Cutting Dovetails

CUTTING DOVETAILS BY HAND involves the same skills as cutting
mortises and tenons. The main
difference is that dovetails are more complex to visualize. This chapter presents the
step-by-step process for cutting through
dovetails, as a means of consolidating and
building upon the skills learned in the previous project.

Whereas mortise-and-tenon joinery is
used primarily for frames, seating, and
other situations in which the end of one
piece of wood butts into the side of
another, dovetails are used for case-piece
construction (boxes, drawers, dressers,
etc.), where two pieces of wood meet at

90° to form a corner. Taken together, the
mortise and tenon and the dovetail form
the cornerstone of traditional wood joinery and are unsurpassed in effectiveness
and quality.

In production work, dovetails can be
cut with a template and router more
quickly than they can by hand. But the
predetermined proportion and regularity
of machined dovetails aesthetically dimin-
ishes the work compared with the har-
monies of spacing and proportion that are
possible with hand-cut dovetails. For the
craftsman building furniture one piece at
a time, handwork is not only aesthetically
superior but also relatively efficient and
far more pleasurable and satisfying.

ANATOMY OF A DOVETAIL

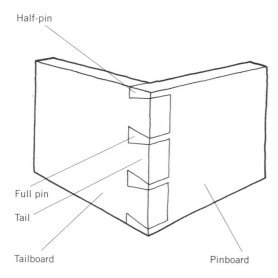

Half-pin

Full pin

Tail

Tailboard

Pinboard

There are infinite combinations of tail and pin thicknesses, spacings, and angles at which dovetails can be cut (see the drawing on p. 109). The choice depends on the maker's aesthetic preference, but tradition provides some guidelines:

- A dovetail joint usually begins and ends with pins. (An exception occurs in traditional drawer construction, as shown on p. 175.) The pins at either end are called "half-pins" because only their interior edges are angled.

- Tail and pin size may vary within a joint, but the tails and pins are usually spaced symmetrically.

- In a wide joint, the outer tails are often smaller than the ones in the middle of the board. Small tails provide greater holding power against cupping.

- The narrowness of pins has traditionally been a way for furniture makers to show off their skill. A good craftsman can cut pins that taper to less than $\frac{1}{16}$ in. at the base, but there is no practical advantage to doing so.

- The angles at which dovetails are cut are traditionally described as 1:6 (one-in-six), 1:7, or 1:8. The steeper degree of physical interlock provided by 1:6 dovetails offers greater mechanical resistance to being pulled apart. The slighter slope of 1:8 dovetails has been thought of as more decorative and pleasing to the eye. Really, dovetails can be cut to any angle within this overall range. Mine are usually between 1:7 and 1:7½.

HOW A ONE-IN-SEVEN ANGLE IS LAID OUT

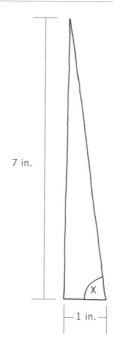

On a piece of paper draw a line 7 in. long and then a line 1 in. long perpendicular to it. Connect the lines to form a triangle and set a sliding T-bevel to angle X.

7 in.

X

1 in.

Cutting Through Dovetails

There are many methods for cutting through dovetails by hand. Woodworkers are an idiosyncratic lot, but we all divide into two basic camps—those who cut tails first and those who begin with pins. My preference is to start with the tails, but I encourage you to experiment with both approaches and make up your own mind.

To prepare for this project, mill a piece of hardwood measuring ⅝ in. by 4 in. by 24 in. and cut it in half to make two pieces with square ends, each about 12 in. long. (Refer back to project 1 on pp. 77–92.) It will be easier to see layout marks on a light-colored wood such as poplar.

The steps we will use to cut through dovetails are shown at top right.

What You'll Need

- ☐ Folding rule
- ☐ Cutting gauge
- ☐ Square
- ☐ Sliding T-bevel
- ☐ Various chisels
- ☐ Dovetail saw
- ☐ Coping saw
- ☐ Draftsman's lead holder and sharpener
- ☐ Block plane or file

What You'll Do

1. Mark the shoulders of the tails and pins.
2. Lay out the tails.
3. Pare back to the tail shoulders.
4. Saw the tails.
5. Chop the shoulders of the tails.
6. Perfect the tails.
7. Lay out the pins, using the tails as a template.
8. Pare back to the pin shoulders.
9. Saw the pins and chop the shoulders.
10. Fit the joint together.
11. Plane the ends flush.

STEP 1 Mark the shoulders of the tails and pins.

First, choose which ends of the two boards will meet to form the joint, and designate one board for tails and the other for pins. Mark the boards with a pencil so you'll remember how they go together. Make sure the ends are square.

To mark the shoulders for the tails and pins, set the cutting gauge to a smidgen more than ⅝ in. from the fence to the blade. Lightly cut a line around all four shoulders, using the end of each board as a reference surface. The lines should be shallow, since they will be visible on the outside of the completed joint where they cross the tails and pins. Some furniture makers leave the lines, especially on drawer sides. Others plane them out once the joint is assembled.

1

WOOD TIP

Through dovetails can be flush or proud. But even when making flush dovetails, the tails and pins are often cut a hair proud to start with and planed flat after assembly. That way, small imperfections left on the board ends from marking, sawing, or chiseling can be eliminated. ■

Mark the shoulders of the tails and pins with a cutting gauge.

STEP 2 Lay out the tails.

You may want to draw a series of possible dovetail variations with pencil and paper before deciding on the final angle and spacing. The base of each tail, and the spaces between them, should be at least as wide as your narrowest chisel (which is probably ¼ in.); otherwise, it will be difficult to clean out the shoulders.

Once you have decided on a pattern, set the angle of a sliding T-bevel to the pitch you have chosen. With a sharp pencil (or an awl or a knife), mark the tails on one face of the designated tailboard. The thinner the pencil lines, the easier it will be to saw precisely. I strongly suggest using a draftsman's lead holder, which you can purchase at any art-supply store along with a little hand-held sharpener.

DOVETAIL VARIATIONS

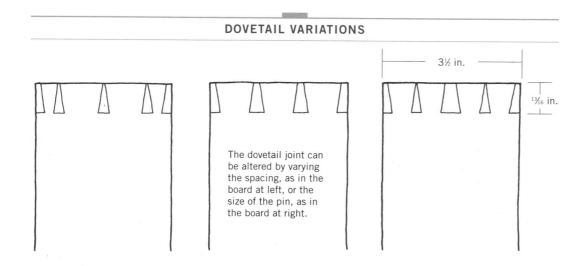

3½ in.

1³⁄₁₆ in.

The dovetail joint can be altered by varying the spacing, as in the board at left, or the size of the pin, as in the board at right.

Lay out the tails with a sliding T-bevel and pencil.

Pare back to the shoulders in the waste areas.

Transfer the lines across the end of the board with a square, then mark them down the other side with the T-bevel. Be careful to align the lines at the edges and to keep your lead sharp.

Finally, boldly mark the waste areas between the tails to avoid mistakes such as sawing to the wrong side of a line. I use a regular or colored pencil for this purpose.

STEP 3 Pare back to the tail shoulders.

Pare a small groove back to the shoulders, from the tail side of the line, in the waste areas between the tails and around the outside edges. This groove will guide the chisel when chopping the shoulders in step 5.

STEP 4 Saw the tails.

To saw the tails, hold the wood upright in a vise. Sawing is easier if you angle the wood enough to make the lines you are cutting vertical. I saw close to the pencil lines but leave just a sliver of wood showing between them and the saw. This makes it easier to saw straight because I see more clearly. Saw down and across simultaneously until you have completed a diagonal cut.

Change the angle of the board to make the other set of tail marks vertical and saw them on the diagonal as well. Then turn the board around in the vise and, with the saw horizontal, saw each set of tail marks down to the shoulder. (When you get good at this, you'll be able to complete each saw cut from the front of the board without turning it around.)

Saw the tails with the board held in a vise.

Use a coping saw to remove waste from between the tails.

Next, use a coping saw to remove as much of the waste as possible from between the tails. Avoid cutting into the tails or shoulders.

STEP 5 Chop the shoulders of the tails.

Place a piece of scrap wood under the work before clamping it in place with bench dogs or clamps. Then chop the shoulders square with a sharp chisel and mallet. If you've left a lot of waste, work your way back to the shoulder in small increments, then use the groove that you pared in step 3 to position the chisel for the final cut. For best results, use the widest chisel that fits.

With a sharp chisel, chop the tail shoulders square.

Chop halfway down. Then turn the board over and chop from the other side. You can expect some tearout as you come down the second side, but it should be invisible in the assembled joint. The angled corners where the tails intersect the shoulders should be cleaned out precisely.

Use the chisel as a straightedge to make sure the shoulders are flat across. The chisel should rest on the outside edges, not rock on a hump in the middle. Slight back-cutting is permissible between the edges.

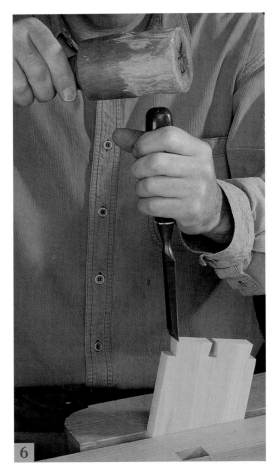

Use a wide chisel and a mallet to square a poorly sawn tail.

^{STEP}**6** Perfect the tails.

Before you mark the pins, it is an excellent practice to perfect the tails so they are square across rather than ragged or crooked. That way all fitting takes place on the pins. The best method to clean up a tail that needs it is as follows:

■ Mark a new line around all three sides just behind the less-than-perfect edge, using your T-bevel and square. Because you are going to mark the pins from whatever tails you end up with, you are not bound by your original layout marks.

■ Place the work upright in a vise so you're working vertically. Chop a clean face on the tail with a wide, sharp chisel. Drive the chisel with light taps from a mallet for maximum control.

■ Use the new line you've marked as a visual reference, but don't cut all the way to it so you can always see it clearly.

■ Keep the back of the chisel firmly against the work as a guide to flatness.

^{STEP}**7** Lay out the pins.

Now that the tails are cleanly cut, you can use them as a template to mark the pins. Place the tailboard flat across a couple of pieces of wood on the benchtop. Clamp the pinboard upright in a face vise so that it butts up against the underside of the tailboard. Align the shoulder of the tails with the inside face of the pinboard.

Trace the tails onto the pinboard with a lead holder, with the lead well extended (or you can use an awl or a knife). This step requires particular attentiveness when the tails are close together.

Once you have traced the tails, remove the tailboard. If your tracings are hard to read, use a straightedge to firm up the marks. Next, carefully square the marks down both faces to the shoulders. Now that the pins are laid out, indicate the waste areas in between with pencil marks.

STEP 8 Pare back to the pin shoulders.

Pare a small groove back to the shoulders in the waste areas between the pins, just as we did on the tailboard in step 3 (see the bottom photo on p. 110).

STEP 9 Cut the pins and chop the shoulders.

Hold the pinboard upright in a vise and cut the pins with a dovetail saw (see the bottom photo at right). Saw them all on the diagonal from the first side, then turn the board around and saw horizontally down to the shoulder. In this case, saw on the waste side up to, but not through, the lines, which are on the part of the pins that should snug up against the tails. The closer you can saw to the lines, the less time you'll have to spend paring back to them later. Remove the waste with a coping saw.

Chop the shoulders, cutting in halfway from each side as in step 5. Make sure the shoulders are straight across and the corners are cleaned out thoroughly.

Use the tails as a template to lay out the pins.

Cut the pins with a dovetail saw.

The assembled dovetail joint, before being trimmed flush.

WOOD TIP

A well-cut dovetail has no visible gaps whatsoever. If the joint does not fit perfectly, there are logical reasons. Problems can be traced to inaccurate marking, inaccurate sawing, or shoulders and edges that have not been pared straight across. ■

STEP **10** Fit the joint together.

Rarely does a dovetail joint fit together perfectly at this point. A certain amount of paring is usually required. The secret here is to *trust your lines*. Before even bothering to fit the joint, make sure that any wood that remains outside the lines you traced on the ends of the pins has been pared away. The sides of the pins should be flat and straight. Most important, *be sure not to remove the lines* themselves. They are golden.

Hold the pins upright in a vise while you attempt to assemble the joint. It should require no greater encouragement than light taps from a rubber mallet. If there are tight spots that require paring, pare only the pins. Theoretically, the tails are already correct.

STEP **11** Plane the ends flush.

The last step is to make the pins and tails flush. Normally, this is done after the joint has been glued together. For the sake of practice, though, you can dispense with the glue. That way, the joint can be pulled apart and the ends cut off for a fresh start.

Hold the assembled joint in a vise and make the joint flush with a sharp block plane and/or a file. Whichever you are using, always work toward the interior of the piece to avoid splintering the wood at the edge.

Plane the tails flush with a block plane, working away from the corner of the joint to avoid splintering.

Don't despair if your first set of dovetails looks something like a smile with some of the teeth missing. Mine certainly did. I gave my first dovetailed box to my grandmother, who took every opportunity to show it off to her friends. A year's practice later, I was so embarrassed by those dovetails that I borrowed the box back and burned it in the fireplace. Unfortunately, my grandmother died before I could make her a new one.

Practice and patience are necessary to master the skill of cutting dovetails. Don't hesitate to cut fresh ends and start again. Mark carefully, use a sharp pencil, and saw with respect for your lines; by the fourth or fifth attempt, the results will begin to please you.

The completed dovetail joint.

PROJECT 4

Building a Small Bench

T HE BENCH PRESENTED in this chapter builds upon the skills learned in previous projects and takes you through the entire furniture-making process, from design to finishing. The bench is joined with half-blind dovetails and through-wedged mortise and tenons.

Feel free to play with the proportions of the bench (the dimensions I used are shown in the top right drawing on the facing page). Maybe you want a wider or longer bench. Is it high enough? Is the stretcher in the right place? Although I hope that you build this first bench with only minor variations, I also encourage you to begin designing your own projects as soon as possible.

THE DESIGN PROCESS

Designing your own furniture is one of the most rewarding aspects of craftsmanship, but even skilled woodworkers sometimes treat furniture design as a mystery on the order of nuclear physics: "Oh, gosh, not me. I can't draw." It's not rocket science, though, believe me!

The design process can begin with something as simple as doodling on a scrap of paper. Doodling is the secret of design inspiration. Extensive doodling often leads to "letting the pencil do the thinking"—a designer's euphemism for a mindless state where ideas seem to appear on paper of their own accord.

Begin with a sketch

Let's say you want to design a small bench to go by your fireplace. Set aside a half-hour or more of undisturbed time, and simply start sketching bench ideas with pencil and paper. Don't worry about drawing ability. You are the only person who has to understand your sketches. Don't stop to evaluate. Keep sketching new variations. If you get stuck, go off in a wildly different direction. After a while you should begin to see some interesting ideas. I sometimes need several sketching sessions to come up with an idea that I want to pursue.

Once you have created one sketch that is particularly appealing, the hard part is done. The rest of the design process consists of translating the sketch into reality by refining the concept and working out the details without sacrificing its charm.

First, decide on the bench's measurements. Examine existing benches as refer-

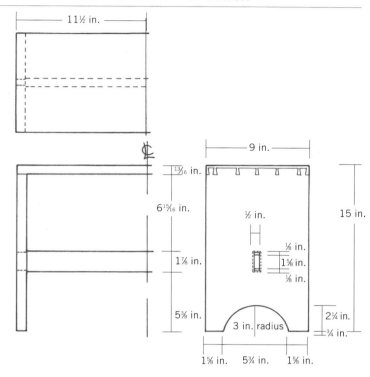

ences for scale and proportion. After a while, design and construction details that ensure function, strength, and durability can be induced from experience. In the meantime, the best way to learn is through observation.

Make a scale drawing

Make scale drawings of your design using a parallel-bar drawing board, a T-square, or even graph paper. An architect's rule makes it easy to work at scales from one-eighth to one-half of life size. Drawing at a scale where ⅛ in. on paper equals 1 in. in real life is appropriate for most furniture, but a small piece such as this bench could also be drawn on a larger scale, such as ¼ in. to 1 in.

SMALL BENCH

Half-blind dovetails

Stretcher

Wedged through tenon

Scale drawings show front and side views, as well as a plan (top) view. All three views are presented flat, without any attempt at creating a sense of perspective. Dotted lines indicate features hidden behind immediate surfaces. If a piece of furniture is symmetrical, you need only draw half the piece, indicating the axis of symmetry with a line labeled "CL" for centerline.

Once you are satisfied with the scale drawing, make a full-scale one that contains all the information required to build the piece. Full-scale drawings are laid out just like scale drawings, with front and side views and a plan view. Draw out every joinery detail to avoid mistakes later. Two advantages of full-scale drawings are that measurements can be taken directly from them and that they can be used to trace templates for curved pieces. They also preserve the information should you ever decide to build the piece again. The only furniture for which I don't make full-scale drawings are pieces that are either too large to fit my drawing board or too simple to require anything more than scale representation. My full-scale drawing board is often a sheet of plywood used in conjunction with a 42-in. T-square.

Making a Cutting List

When a design has been worked out through full-scale drawings, the next step is to make a cutting list to indicate the finished size of each component. Be sure that when you figure the length of a piece you include tenons or other joinery that may extend beyond the shoulders. The standard format for indicating the size of a piece of wood is to list thickness first, width second, and length third.

In the process of milling components out of rough lumber, pieces are generally cut to final thickness and width, but left an inch or so longer than indicated on the cutting list until it's time to use them. This is because, as you build a piece of furniture, distances between components can change due to small mistakes.

CUTTING LIST FOR SMALL BENCH

- ☐ 1 piece at $1\frac{3}{16}$ in. x 9 in. x $23\frac{1}{16}$ in. (bench top, including $\frac{1}{32}$-in. waste at each end)

- ☐ 2 pieces at $1\frac{3}{16}$ in. x 9 in. x $14\frac{3}{4}$ in. (legs, exact length)

- ☐ 1 piece at $1\frac{3}{16}$ in. x $1\frac{7}{8}$ in. x $23\frac{1}{8}$ in. (stretcher, including through tenons with $\frac{1}{16}$ in. to spare at either end)

Selecting the Lumber

Criteria for choosing the species of wood for a project can include color, grain, strength, cost, and availability. Some furniture makers like to mix different woods together; others prefer to use a single species per piece. Some like the contrast provided by sapwood; others use only heartwood.

My own preference has been to work from a palette of domestic hardwoods: cherry, ash, maple, oak, and walnut. Among these woods I can almost always find a color and grain pattern to complement the design I am working on. The lighter-colored woods (ash, oak, and maple) are more casual. Walnut has an air of formality. The pronounced grains of ash and oak emphasize the woodiness of a piece, whereas the finer grains of maple and cherry compete less with the form. All five woods are strong, but oak and ash are more supple where steam bending is involved.

My favorite wood is cherry, which has an informal elegance that harmonizes with my idea of domesticity. Neither too light nor too dark, the fine grain lets you know it is wood without shouting about it. Cherry works cleanly and crisply, with relatively little tendency to tear out, and the small pores take finish well.

Once you have chosen a species for your bench, select the board or boards you will use. Where possible, take an entire piece of furniture out of one board, or

Decisions, Decisions

Before cutting the wood for this project, you have a number of decisions to make:

1 Can the full width of the bench come out of one board?

2 Do you want to cut the pieces sequentially out of a single board so that the grain pattern continues up one leg, along the top, and down the other leg?

3 Which section of the board has the symmetry, pattern, and color to make the most attractive bench top?

4 Are sapwood and knots acceptable?

5 Will the first face be flattened with a jointer or a handplane? Even if the board is too wide for the capacity of your jointer, it can be ripped in half, joined, thicknessed, and glued back together again, as explained on pp. 120–124.

boards from the same tree, so the color and grain will match throughout.

All four parts of the bench are drawn to be $\frac{13}{16}$ in. thick, which you should be able to get out of 4/4 roughsawn lumber. However, if the wood starts off significantly warped and you end up with a tad less than $\frac{13}{16}$ in. by the time it's milled flat, that's what you work with.

Whatever wood you choose, look it over for surface cracks, end checks, sapwood, knots, bow, cup, and twist (see pp. 8–9). No craftsman ever finds a perfect board; we do the best we can with what we have.

MILLING THE LUMBER

Once you have answered the questions in the sidebar on p.119, mark the rough lumber, cut it in sections, and mill it four-square to final thickness and width. Milling the stretcher involves the same straightforward process we encountered in project 1 (see pp. 77–92). The benchtop and legs can be more challenging because, if you are taking them out of a single board, they are too wide for the 6-in. and 8-in. jointers found in most small shops.

There are two standard ways to deal with flattening a board that is too wide for your jointer. You can either handplane the first face flat and then run the second face through a thickness planer, or you can rip the board into narrower components that fit your jointer, put them through the milling process, and then glue them back together. The first method has the advantage of avoiding gluelines and gives the nicest appearance. The second method requires less skill.

The photos on pp.122–123 show the "handplane" method. First, the components are cut to roughly 1 in. longer than the finished dimension and ripped on the bandsaw to approximate width. Next, one face of each board is handplaned flat. Then the other face is machined flat in the thickness planer, one edge is squared on the jointer, the board is cut to final width on a table saw, and the ends are crosscut square and to length with a sliding table on the table saw.

When you remove wood from the surface of a wide board, it often changes the moisture equilibrium between the two faces and causes the wood to warp. In order to minimize this problem, I generally stop thickness planing when the wood is about ³⁄₃₂ in. over final thickness and let it sit overnight (or longer) exposed to air on both sides. When I come back to the wood the next day, I check it for flatness and, if it has cupped or twisted, re-plane one face. Then I take the wood to final dimension with the thickness planer and complete the milling process.

The basic steps involved in the "jointer" method of milling wide boards are as follows (you would follow the same process, minus steps 2 and 3, if you were working with narrow boards from the start):

1 Cut the rough wood to approximate lengths.

2 Make distinctive marks on the end of each board so that it will be easy to know which halves go together at the conclusion of the milling process.

WOOD TIP

When milling boards that are to be glued together to make a wider panel that will still fit my thickness planer, I generally prefer to leave them about ³⁄₃₂ in. thicker and a little wider than finished dimension. Then, after they are glued, I have the option of touching up one face of the panel with a handplane, if necessary, before machining the wood to final thickness, width, and length. This enables me to correct for any cupping that occurs, as well as for less-than-perfect alignment between glued edges. ∎

3 Saw the boards in half lengthwise, preferably with a bandsaw or hand ripsaw. Ripping rough lumber to width on the table saw may be common practice, but it's not such a good idea (see pp. 80–81).

4 Flatten the first face of each piece on the jointer.

5 Thickness-plane both boards to final thickness. (See the sidebar on the facing page for a refinement of this process.)

6 Use the jointer to square the inside edge of each board—the edges that meet when the board is reassembled. (You can compensate for an imperfectly squared jointer fence by running the face of one board and the back of the other against it. When the boards are reassembled, any variation from 90° imparted by the jointer will, in effect, cancel itself out.)

7 Cut both boards to a width of 4½ in. on the table saw, so that their combined width is 9 in.

8 Glue the two boards back together, making sure their surfaces line up flush, and let the glue dry overnight.

9 Cut the reassembled board to length on the table saw.

If you choose to follow the "jointer" method of milling outlined above, you should read the section on gluing and assembly (see pp. 142–146), as well as the following notes:

When edge-gluing two boards together, support the work at a height where the screw thread aligns with the center of the board.

- To line up edges while gluing, some woodworkers insert dowels, splines, or biscuits. I usually take the riskier (and faster) road of aligning the edges by hand as I clamp the boards together. Occasionally, glue sets before the boards are in position, but most of the time everything works out fine.

- Boards tend to arch under the pressure of clamping when their edges aren't square, the wood is thin, or the clamps have too much flex. If possible, glue wide panels together with bar clamps, which distort the least in tension. To keep panels flat, it helps to position the

MILLING THE LEGS AND TOP

A SIGNIFICANT CHARACTERISTIC of furniture making is that each step builds on the quality of what has gone before, which is to say that it is much easier to cut accurate joinery if you are working with flat, straight, square stock. So take your time, pay attention to the details, and enjoy milling your work.

2 Bandsaw the board to approximate width if necessary.

1 Cut the roughsawn board to approximate length with a circular saw.

3 Plane the first face flat, starting with a scrub plane if necessary.

4 **Thickness-plane the second face of the board.**

5 **Joint one edge of the board square to the first face.**

6 **Rip the board to finished width on the table saw.**

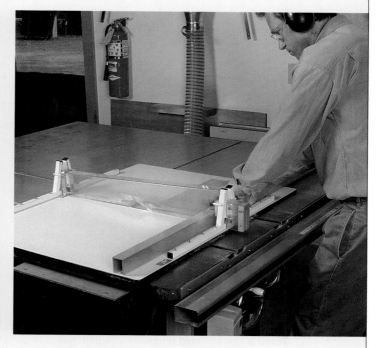

7 **Crosscut the board to finished length using a sliding table on the table saw.**

work so that the screw thread of the clamp delivers pressure straight through the center of the wood (see the bottom photo on p. 121). Another trick is to hold glued and clamped boards flat between pairs of sticks clamped across them.

■ Newly glued boards should be left alone for a day or two before smoothing the joint. If moisture introduced by glue hasn't had time to evaporate, the wood along the joint will shrink in thickness as it dries, creating a depression.

At the conclusion of the milling process, you will have four four-square pieces of wood cut to the sizes indicated on the cutting list. The legs and top can be trimmed to their final lengths at this point, but the stretcher should be left a little long until it's time to cut the tenons. The ends where dovetails are to be cut should be as square across as possible.

CUTTING HALF-BLIND DOVETAILS

Depending on your aesthetic preference, you can join the legs to the benchtop with either through or half-blind dovetails. I designed this bench with half-blind dovetails because I like the way they leave the top surface uninterrupted. If you are cutting half-blind dovetails for the first time, I suggest practicing on scrap wood before you get to the real thing.

What You'll Need

- ☐ Cutting gauge
- ☐ Folding rule
- ☐ Knife
- ☐ Sharp pencil
- ☐ Dovetail saw
- ☐ Square
- ☐ Various chisels
- ☐ Mallet
- ☐ Sliding T-bevel
- ☐ Drill
- ☐ Brad-point bits in various sizes

STEP 1 Orient the legs and the top.

Place the parts of the bench in their relative positions and mark them with a pencil so there will be no confusion as to how they go together.

STEP 2 Mark the tail shoulders.

Set a sharp cutting gauge to scribe the shoulders of the dovetails on the legs. The

What You'll Do

1. Orient the legs and the top.
2. Mark the tail shoulders.
3. Lay out the tails.
4. Pare back to the tail shoulders.
5. Saw the tails and chop the shoulders.
6. Mark the pin shoulders.
7. Mark the pin depth.
8. Lay out the pins from the tails.
9. Pare back to the pin shoulders.
10. Saw the pins.
11. Drill out the waste.
12. Chop the shoulders and pare the waste.
13. Fit the joints.

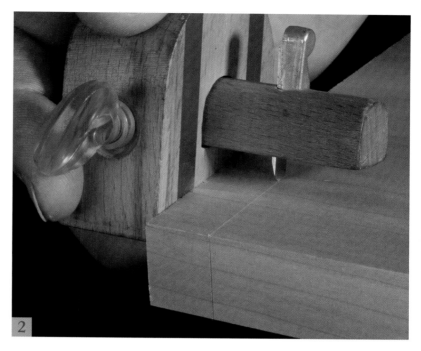

Mark the shoulders on the legs with a cutting gauge set to ⅝ in.

length of the tails must allow for the "web," the thickness of wood that will remain between them and the top surface of the bench. If the bench stock is ¹³⁄₁₆ in. thick and you plan to leave a ³⁄₁₆-in.-thick web, the gauge should be set to mark ⅝-in.-long tails.

Marking and cutting the dovetails for both ends of the bench at the same time increases efficiency. Lightly mark the shoulders around all four sides of both legs, holding the fence of the cutting gauge against the ends of the boards. This light scribe line will be deepened later in the waste areas. Where it crosses the base of the tails, the line will be planed off after assembly.

Save the setting on the cutting gauge to mark the pins.

PARTS OF A PINBOARD

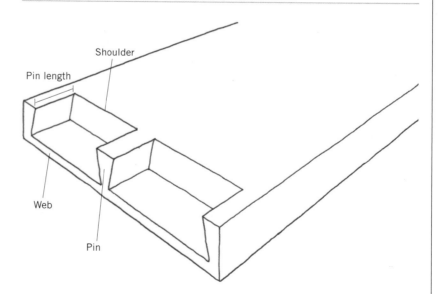

Shoulder

Pin length

Web

Pin

Use a sliding T-bevel to lay out the tails.

Transfer the layout of the tails from one leg to the other.

3 Lay out the tails.

Lay out the tails in a pattern that pleases you. Refer to the guidelines on pp. 109–110. This is where my friend Jim Krenov says you can either make music or make noise. When the tails on one leg have been marked around both sides and the end, transfer their spacing to the other leg by squaring the end marks across. Be sure to identify waste areas clearly with bold pencil marks.

STEP 4 Pare back to the tail shoulders.

Use the cutting gauge to knife the shoulder lines more deeply in the areas where waste will be removed. Pare back to the shoulders from the waste side to form small, straight-backed grooves.

Pare back to the shoulders between the tails.

Use a backsaw to saw
the tails.

STEP **5** Saw the tails and chop the shoulders.

Saw the tails with a dovetail saw and chop out the waste areas, as explained on pp. 110–112.

STEP **6** Mark the pin shoulders.

Mark the shoulders for the pins with a knife and square. Pin shoulders are marked only on the bottom side of the bench top. Each pin shoulder should be set in from the end of the board a hair deeper than the thickness of a leg, so that the pins end up slightly proud and can be planed flush after assembly.

Mark the shoulders for the pins on the bottom side of the bench top.

Scribe the pin depth with the cutting gauge.

STEP 7 Mark the pin depth.

With the cutting gauge at the same setting used to scribe the length of the dovetails, mark the depth of the pins. Place the fence of the gauge against the underside of the bench top and scribe a line across each end.

STEP 8 Lay out the pins from the tails.

Use the tails as a template to mark the pins, as described on pp. 112–113, but this time, instead of aligning the inside shoulders of the boards, align the top of the leg with the cutting gauge line you just made across the end of the bench top. Because these are half-blind dovetails, the pins are squared down the bottom face of the board only. Mark the waste areas between the pins with a bold pencil.

Use the tailboard as a template to lay out the pins.

Saw the pins on the diagonal.

STEP 9 Pare back to the pin shoulders.

Pare back to the shoulders in the waste areas between the pins.

STEP 10 Saw the pins.

Using a dovetail saw, cut the pins on the diagonal, from the shoulder to the depth mark. Saw on the waste side of the pins; saw right up to the pencil (or scribe) line, but make sure it's still there when you're done or there will be gaps in the joint.

STEP 11 Drill out the waste.

Use a drill press or hand drill to remove most of the waste between the pins. If you are using a drill press, set the depth stop to a hair less than the finished depth of the pins. If you are using a hand drill, you can wrap masking tape around the bit as a depth indicator.

Drill out the bulk of the waste between the pins.

Working with the chisel parallel to the workbench, pare out the waste between the pins.

STEP **12** Chop the shoulders
and pare the waste.

At this point, clamp the pinboard on the
bench top about 2 in. in from the edge.
This allows you to pare the pin bottoms
nice and straight by keeping the chisel
parallel to the bench.

Begin by chopping a false shoulder
about 1/16 in. in from the real one, so that
you can pry out waste without denting the
real shoulder. Next, split out the waste,

from the end, with a chisel and mallet. Don't try to get it all out in one chunk; work your way down about ⅛ in. at a time. Before you reach the bottom, clean out all interior corners. When the corners are clear, chop the final shoulder and pare the true bottom.

Finally, hold the bench top vertical in a vise and pare the sides of the pins so that a chisel will rest flat against both visible edges. Remember, pare up to your pencil (or scribe) lines, but trust your marks and leave them intact.

The completed pins should have crisp interior corners and flat sides. Shoulders and bottoms can be slightly undercut for an easier fit, if necessary.

STEP 13 Fit the joints.

Try to assemble the dovetails. Moderate tapping with a deadblow mallet should provide sufficient force. Too tight a fit may split the wood during assembly, so take your time assessing tight spots. If the tails are already cleanly cut and square across, all paring should take place on the pins.

When both dovetail joints fit to your satisfaction, disassemble them in preparation for the next step—cutting the through-wedged mortise-and-tenon joints. Leave the pins proud for now. They will not be planed flush until the bench has been glued together.

The assembled joint will be cleaned up after the bench components have been glued together.

CUTTING THE THROUGH-WEDGED MORTISE AND TENONS

I designed this bench with through-wedged mortise-and-tenon joints connecting the stretcher to the legs. Wedges spread the ends of the tenons to make them tighter in the mortises. Before reliable glues existed, dependable tenons had to be locked in place mechanically with pegs or wedges. These days, pegs and wedges are often employed more for appearance than for utility.

The process of cutting a through-wedged mortise and tenon is essentially the same as that used to cut a blind mortise and tenon (see pp. 93–105). The following instructions emphasize those parts of the process that differ.

STEP 1 Mark out the mortise.

The through mortises must be accurately marked on both sides of each leg. Begin by squaring fine pencil lines, 1⅛ in. apart, around one of the boards to locate the top and bottom of the mortise. Then transfer these lines to the second leg and square them around it, too.

Next, scribe the mortise thickness (½ in.) on both sides of both legs. Mark from consistent edges—that is, from edges of both legs that face the same way when the bench is assembled. This prevents the mortises from being offset if they aren't perfectly centered.

If you use a mortise gauge, save the setting between the pins for marking the tenons later. If your mortise gauge doesn't reach in far enough, you may be able to scribe the mortises with a marking gauge or a cutting gauge at two different settings. In this case, for consistency, you would mark a line on both sides of both legs at the first setting, then do the same at the second setting. If none of your gauges have a long enough reach, alternative methods of marking the mortises include carefully squaring fine pencil lines lengthwise around the legs.

Once the mortise thickness is established, re-mark the mortise ends on all sides with a knife and square.

STEP 2 Pare back to the knife lines.

See pp. 96–97.

STEP 3 Drill out the waste.

The cautious approach is to drill halfway in from each side of the workpiece with a ⅜-in. or ⁷⁄₁₆-in. brad-point bit. Drilling all the way through from one side risks tearing out the other where the bit pushes through. If you choose to drill all the way through, place the work on top of a piece of scrap to keep the bit from coming through into empty space.

STEP 4 Chop down just shy of the ends.

Chop down about ¹⁄₁₆ in. in from the mortise ends. Work from both sides to meet in the middle (see p. 98–99).

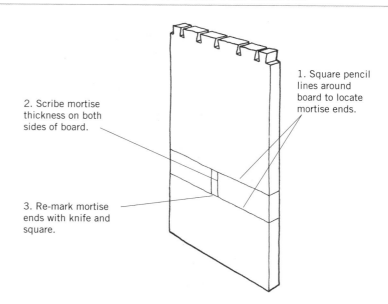

MARKING THE THROUGH MORTISE

1. Square pencil lines around board to locate mortise ends.

2. Scribe mortise thickness on both sides of board.

3. Re-mark mortise ends with knife and square.

STEP 5 Pare the mortise cheeks and remove waste.

Gradually work your way down both cheeks with a chisel and mallet, from both sides, until the mortises are cleaned out. If you marked the mortise thickness with pencil lines, you may want to scribe over the line with an awl to provide a starting groove for the chisel.

STEP 6 Chop the ends to the knife lines.

Chop the ends of the mortises at the knife lines, working down from both sides to meet in the middle (see p. 100).

STEP 7 Pare the mortise cheeks and ends square.

The cheeks of the mortises should be flat. They are the long-grain glue surfaces within the joint and need to make close contact with the cheeks of the tenons. The mortise ends, which are end grain, are less critical and can be slightly back-cut.

STEP 8 Mark the tenon shoulders.

Place the stretcher lengthwise on the underside of the bench top. Since the stretcher has been left a little longer than necessary, it should project beyond both ends of the top. Use a knife to transfer the shoulder marks of the pins to the stretcher, thereby establishing the locations of the tenon shoulders. Square the shoulders around all four sides of the stretcher with a knife.

Measure the desired tenon length out from each shoulder. A flush through tenon should be about 1/32 in. proud until it is planed after glue-up. If your tenon is going to stay proud, it should be cut to finished length at this point. Square a line around each tenon end and saw it to length.

STEP 9 Scribe the tenon thickness.

If you scribed the mortise thickness with a mortise gauge, maintain the setting between the pins, but adjust the fence to center the tenon on the end of the stretcher.

If you laid out the mortise by an alternative method, set the pins of the mortise gauge against the width of the actual mortise. Adjust the fence to center the tenon on the stretcher. Register the gauge against a consistent face of the stretcher at both ends to avoid offset tenons.

STEP 10 Mark the tenon width.

See p. 102. The tenons on this bench are 1⅝ in. wide, centered between two ⅛-in. shoulders.

Wedge kerfs are cut in the tenon to house the wedges, which are inserted when the joint is assembled.

16

STEP 11 Pare back to the shoulders.

See pp. 102-103.

STEP 12 Saw the shoulders with a backsaw.

See pp. 103-104.

STEP 13 Saw the cheeks.

See p. 104.

STEP 14 Re-mark and saw the width.

Saw the tenon width straight and true because the end of the tenon will be visible in the assembled joint.

STEP 15 Clean up and fit.

Fit the tenons to the mortises. The cheeks should mate perfectly. Any gap at the top or bottom should be taken up when the wedges are driven in. If the tenons are to remain proud, rather than be planed flush, this is a good time to clean up the end grain, which will be difficult to work after assembly. Break the edges slightly around both ends, smooth the ends with a block plane or file, followed by sandpaper on a sanding block, and then sand the broken edges to a uniform appearance.

STEP 16 Cut the wedge slots.

A wedge should be oriented to spread a tenon against the end grain of the mortise. Pressure against the long grain could split the wood around the mortise. Make two saw kerfs in the tenons, no more than

RIGHT AND WRONG WAYS TO WEDGE A THROUGH TENON

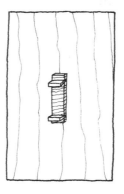

Right way: Wedges exert pressure against the end grain of the mortise.

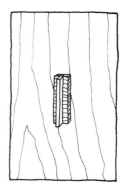

Wrong way: Wedges exert pressure against the edge grain of the mortise.

¼ in. from each tenon edge, as shown in the photo on the facing page. Use a bandsaw or a thick-kerfed backsaw. A tablesaw kerf is too wide and a fine dovetail saw kerf too narrow.

STEP 17 Make the wedges.

For color contrast, wedges are often made from a different wood than the rest of the piece. I chose walnut wedges for this cherry bench.

To make the wedges, mill a small piece of wood to fit the thickness of the mortise (½ in.) and cut narrow, thinly tapered wedges along the grain with a bandsaw or backsaw. Trim the thin end off of each wedge with a chisel so that it enters only about ⅛ in. into the kerf without pressure. This will enable the wedge to impart the maximum spread to the tenon before bottoming out in the slot when you assemble the bench.

17

Saw wedges from a long piece of contrasting wood that has been milled to a thickness equal to the width of the mortise. That way, the wedges will automatically be the right width.

When you test-fit the joint, don't drive the wedges in—you would never get them out. Cut extra wedges in case you lose or break some in the hurry of gluing.

Making the leg cutouts

The shape of the cutout is an arc of a circle with a 3-in. diameter, centered ⅝ in. below the bottom of the leg, as shown in the scale drawing on p. 117. This shape works for me, but you might test a few different shapes to see what pleases you. An easy way to do so is to tape on paper cutouts.

When you have decided on a design, mark it on each leg with a compass, a template, or any other method that yields a thin, precise pencil line. A curve such as the arc I've drawn may be cut with a bandsaw fitted with a ¼-in. blade or with a coping saw.

Make the sawn curve fair and smooth with a half-round wood file. Begin by filing slight bevels along the edges to prevent splintering. Then, using the flat side of the file, work with the grain, from the center of the leg up toward the sides.

EDGE TREATMENT

Edges can be shaped in infinite variation, from the simplicity of a hard edge to the formality of a Roman ogee.

The point in the furniture-making process at which an edge should be formed varies. Sometimes it's easier before glue-up, sometimes after. The simple, broken edge (slightly rounded or chamfered) on our bench is more easily accomplished after the piece has been glued together. However, the edges of the stretcher should be treated now, while they are fully accessible. (For a discussion of breaking the edges, see p. 145.)

EDGE TREATMENTS

Hard edge

Chamfer

Quarter-round

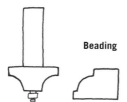

Beading

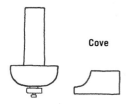

Cove

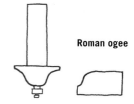

Roman ogee

Routed edges are cut with self-guiding bits—cutters that have bearings attached to limit their penetration. Edges can be molded on a router table or freehand.

Surface preparation

Once the joinery has been cut, the bench is about halfway to completion. The remaining steps are surface preparation, gluing, and finishing.

Surface preparation is the process of removing any nicks, tearout, pencil lines, scratches, and other imperfections to leave a consistently smooth, clean surface ready to take a finish. Where possible, surface preparation is begun prior to gluing, while the components are still separate and easy to work with. Though surface preparation can be the most tedious part of furniture making, patience and a watchful eye are rewarded. The more care you invest, the clearer and deeper the grain will appear when the finish is applied.

There are three ways to prepare a surface—sanding, planing, and scraping—and they can be used singly or in combination. There is no right or wrong method; you just find what works for you. And your methods may vary depending on the type of wood or the design of your project.

To complete the job entirely with sandpaper, you would begin with relatively coarse paper such as 100 grit, sanding until all defects were removed and the sur-face bore a uniform scratch pattern. Then, grit by grit, you would work your way up to 220 grit or even higher, at each step replacing the scratches left by the previous grit with the finer scratch pattern of the current grit. This is a surefire method, if done meticulously, but it is also a tedious and dusty way to spend your time.

At the other end of the scale, hand-planing is potentially the most time-efficient method of surface preparation and can leave the most desirable surface. A sharp blade slices wood so cleanly that any two adjacent points on a planed surface are (theoretically) in the same geometric plane, which means that they reflect light at the same angle. Because you get so much visual information from the wood, you see the grain with the greatest possible depth and clarity. By way of contrast, picture a sanded surface, where the scratch pattern of tiny ridges and valleys reflects light every which way. Unfortunately, a handplaned surface is difficult to achieve without incurring at least a small amount of tearout, and few furniture makers attempt it successfully.

In a way, scraping is a compromise between planing and sanding. A scraper takes shavings without the risk of tearout, so it is quicker than sanding and lets you avoid working with the coarser grits. But scraped wood tends to be fuzzier than handplaned wood, so some sanding with the finer grits is still necessary.

The specific process of surface preparation that I suggest using on the bench is as follows:

1 Remove all visible flaws with a hand scraper.

2 Sand with 150-grit sandpaper.

3 Glue the piece together and let the glue dry overnight.

4 Clean up the joints and plane the edges flush.

5 Scrape the areas you've just worked on.

6 Sand all as-yet-unsanded surfaces with 150-grit paper.

7 Break the edges.

8 Dampen the surface of the wood with water to raise the grain. Allow the wood to dry overnight.

9 Sand with 220-grit paper until all surfaces are smooth again.

10 Apply the finish.

Scraping

A hand scraper is a thin, rectangular piece of soft steel. A hooked burr, formed along the edge with a piece of harder steel, takes fine shavings without tearout, even when scraping against the grain.

The thickness of a scraper is important. If it's too thin, it will heat up quickly and burn your fingers. If it's too thick, it will lack the requisite flexibility. Scrapers made by Sandvik, Lie-Nielsen Toolworks, and Two Cherries are among the best. They measure approximately 0.80 mm thick by 2½ in. wide by 6 in. long.

Preparing a scraper edge is an art in itself. Step-by-step instructions are given in the sidebar on pp. 140–141.

To use a scraper, hold it with the hook down and facing away from you. Grasp the ends with both hands, and place your

To use a scraper, hold it upright with both hands and push it away from you along the grain of the board. If the scraper was sharpened correctly (see pp. 140–141), it should take a clean shaving.

thumbs in the middle to provide some flex. Push the scraper away from you, slightly flexed, along the grain. At an almost upright angle, the hook should bite and take a good shaving.

Scrapers do not stay sharp for long—instead of shavings they begin to make dust. You can resharpen several times by repeating steps 4 to 6 in the sidebar on pp. 140–141. After a while, though, you will want to put on a new edge, beginning with step 1.

Scrape all the long-grain surfaces of the bench, except in areas that will affect the fit of the joinery. Avoid the wood around each mortise where the tenon shoulders make contact. Similarly, avoid the pins and tails. Scrape until all dings, plane marks, and tearout are gone. The surface should have an even quality.

Sanding

Sand the scraped surfaces to a uniform degree of abrasion, again avoiding the joints. I usually go straight from the scraper to 150-grit or finer sandpaper, but you may prefer 120 grit, especially if you haven't fully mastered the art of scraping.

Sand by hand or with a random-orbital disk sander or an orbital sander (see pp. 54–55). The correct way to use one of these machine sanders is to move it slowly in line with the grain without significant hand pressure.

To sand by hand, wrap the sandpaper around a sanding block for greater efficiency, a flatter surface, and reduced abrasion of your fingertips. You can purchase cork, foam, or rubber-based sanding blocks, or make your own out of similar materials. Always sand with the grain. Cross-grain scratches are extremely visible and difficult to remove.

When you have uniformly sanded the scraped surfaces with 150-grit open-coat aluminum oxide sandpaper, the bench is ready for assembly.

SANDPAPER

Sandpapers are classified according to the type and coarseness of the abrasive. The standard abrasive for wood, in grits up to 220, is open-coat aluminum oxide, which is usually tan or orange colored. Another abrasive, silicon carbide, is used to make the gray, wet/dry sandpaper used in the finishing process.

PREPARING A HAND SCRAPER

THERE ARE MANY VARIATIONS on the basic method of preparing a scraper edge, and different degrees of perfection are suitable for different applications. For example, the coarse edge created by a file is great for removing paint and glue. A more polished edge cuts more efficiently and leaves a smoother surface on wood, which is desirable in preparation for finishing.

Generally, only the two long edges of the scraper are "sharpened." First, they are flattened and squared with a file and honed on stones. Then they are formed into hooks with a burnisher.

The specific steps for preparing a hand scraper are as follows:

1 File the edge straight and square with a mill file. An 8-in. mill bastard works fine, but a slightly finer file, such as an 8-in.

mill second-cut, is better because it leaves smaller scratches behind. Try to do this work away from your workbench—metal filings that find their way into wood will eventually oxidize and form gray spots.

2 Hone the filed edge, first on a medium-grit stone to remove the file scratches, then on a fine stone. Hold the scraper perfectly upright to keep the edge square. Avoid wearing a groove in the stone.

3 Hold the scraper flat on a fine stone to hone the sides. The first time you do this with a new scraper, you'll need to begin on a medium stone, such as a 1,000-grit waterstone, and hone until the entire side has been affected where it meets the edge. Then move on to your fine stone, which is all that will be needed for subsequent sharpenings.

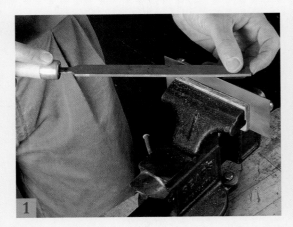

1

With the scraper held firmly in a vise, create a clean edge with a mill file.

2

Hone the edges of the scraper on a medium-grit stone first (as shown), then on a fine stone.

Hone the sides of the scraper on a fine stone.

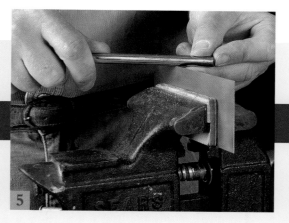

Pull any burr off with a burnisher held flat on the face of the scraper.

Stroke the edge of the scraper with the burnisher held at 90°. Then repeat with the burnisher at a slight angle.

Imagine you are forcing the scraper edge outward into a burr. Move the burnisher along the length and across the edge in a single motion, then do the same thing in the other direction so that you form burrs on both sides of each long edge. Just a few hard strokes in each direction should do the trick.

6 Repeat the previous step with the burnisher held slightly (about 5°) off vertical. Imagine you are forming the burr you have just raised into a slight hook. The scraper should now be ready to use. If not, go back to step 4 and try again (assuming that you got a shaving at the end of step 3, so we know you're dealing with a sharp edge in the first place).

When you have completed step 3, the scraper should be sharp enough to take a good test shaving. If it's not, start again at step 1. In steps 4 through 6 you will deform this sharp edge into a hook that cuts even more aggressively and efficiently.

4 Place the scraper flat on the benchtop. Pull off any burr or hook with the burnisher held flat on top of the scraper. The burnisher is pulled along and off the edge in one motion.

5 Hold the scraper upright in a vise. Stroke along the edge with the burnisher held horizontal at 90°. Press hard.

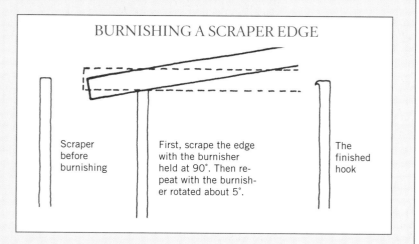

BURNISHING A SCRAPER EDGE

Scraper before burnishing

First, scrape the edge with the burnisher held at 90°. Then repeat with the burnisher rotated about 5°.

The finished hook

Gluing and Assembly

Gluing is the one part of furniture making where there is do-or-die time pressure. The second piece of furniture that I built was a rocking chair. I was too inexperienced to realize that I could either use a slow-setting glue or glue it together in stages, so a friend and I tried to assemble the entire chair at one go with ordinary yellow glue. As we frantically pounded joints together and tightened clamps, the glue began to set. We redoubled our efforts, close to panic. Finally, everything was tightly together except the lowest stretcher between the back legs. The glue had set with one of the tenons only partially inserted, and neither clamping nor hammering would budge it. To this day, wherever that chair may be, there is still a ¼-in. gap at the tenon shoulder.

Preparation is the key to successful gluing. Always do a test run. Dry-clamp the bench without glue to be sure that every joint fits correctly, that the clamps are ready, and that the necessary cauls are cut. (However, don't drive in the wedges until the actual glue-up.)

A caul is a piece of wood used to direct the pressure of clamps and/or to protect the work from clamp jaws. For clamping the bench, a pair of special cauls should be cut to press the tails home around the pins. Another pair of cauls, straight and flat, help to press the mortises and tenons together.

Know Your Glue

There are many types of glue available, including white, yellow, plastic resin, polyurethane, hide, and epoxy. They vary in setting time, drying time, water resistance, ease of cleanup, color, toxicity, elasticity, durability, and bonding characteristics.

The best general-purpose glue for woodworking is yellow (aliphatic-resin) glue. Sold under such names as Titebond and Carpenter's Glue, ordinary yellow glue is nontoxic, cleans up easily with water, and provides a bond stronger than the internal one between wood fibers. Yellow glue bonds best between wood surfaces that are in contact with one another. It doesn't hold well across gaps in the way that epoxy and plastic resin do.

For multiple laminations and other complex assemblies, a slower-setting glue such as plastic resin might be more appropriate than yellow glue. For outdoor furniture, where water resistance is a factor, there are a number of glues to choose from, including water-resistant yellow glue, epoxy, resorcinol, and polyurethane. Research to find the glue that fits your particular needs.

After dry-clamping successfully, gather the following materials in preparation for the actual glue-up:

Before glue-up, dry-clamp the bench with cauls in place to make sure that all the joints fit together correctly.

- Glue. For edge joints I prefer to apply glue from a squeeze bottle. But for assembling joinery, as we are doing here, I prefer to keep glue in a small, wide-mouthed jar (or pour some in a yogurt container) and spread it with a brush.

- Brushes. A small, stiff brush is best for spreading glue in and around joints. I generally use the cheap "acid brushes" sold for plumbers at hardware stores. For edge gluing, where more glue needs to be spread, I recommend that you buy an inexpensive 1-in. paintbrush and cut the bristles short for stiffness.

- A small bucket of clean water for washing glue off the wood and cleaning brushes.

CAUL FOR PRESSING THE DOVETAIL HOME

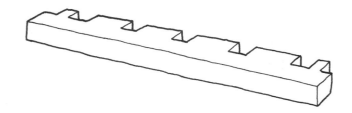

- A white cotton rag for washing glue off the wood.

- A deadblow mallet for knocking the joints together.

- A friend. An extra set of hands helps to spread glue quickly and to put on clamps and cauls.

- A hammer and wood block. Have a hammer on standby in case of emergency; you may need it to drive a joint home or break one apart. The wood block is to protect the furniture from hammer dents. In the case of our bench, a hammer is needed to drive the wedges into the tenon.

There is no need to apply glue to end grain, but spread glue quickly and evenly over all mating, long-grain surfaces within every joint. If only one surface within a joint is coated with yellow glue, the wood can suck the water out of the glue so quickly that not enough will be left to transfer into the second surface upon assembly, resulting in a weak, "glue-starved" joint.

Once the glue is spread, assemble the bench. Attach the top and stretcher to one of the legs, then put the other leg into place. Knock the joints together with the deadblow mallet. Force them home with cauls and clamps. The cauls for the stretcher joints should be placed just below the mortises to allow access to the wedge slots. Maintain even clamp pressure on both sides of the mortises to avoid damaging the legs or gluing them askew.

When the joints have been clamped so the shoulders pull up tight, spread glue on the wedges, manually start both wedges into each tenon, then drive them with the hammer. When two wedges go into one tenon, as they do on our bench, they must be driven in gradually and evenly, with alternating hammer taps from wedge to wedge. Otherwise the first one in will take up all the available space.

When the bench is fully assembled, make sure the legs are square to the bench top. The most likely problem is that excessive clamp pressure has bowed the top. If so, simply ease off on the clamps.

Wash off any visible glue with a stiff brush and rag, especially where it has squeezed out of interior corners. I use an acid brush that I have cut short with a pair of scissors to make the bristles stiffer. Leave the clamps on for at least half an hour. Let the glue dry overnight before going on to the next step.

Cleaning up the joints

Through tenons can be left proud or planed flush. Begin by sawing off the protruding wedges with a backsaw. If the

WOOD TIP

When planing end grain, there is a danger that the edges will splinter off as the blade leaves the wood. On a proud tenon, paring a bevel along the edges solves the problem and makes a nice detail. If your dovetails are less than perfect and you want to prevent edge-splintering as you plane toward the gaps, first score around the base of the pins with a knife. They will break cleanly at the knife cut instead of below the surface of the leg. ■

The wedged tenon will be trimmed flush once the glue has dried.

tenons are proud, clean up the end with a file or block plane and a sanding block. If the tenons are to be flush, take them down completely with a block plane, then scrape and sand the surface as you did the rest of the bench. Similarly, the protruding pins of the dovetail joints should be planed or filed flush, then scraped and sanded.

If the edges of the legs are not already flush with those of the top, plane them flush with the block plane or a bench plane.

Once the joints, edges, and corners are cleaned up, scrape and sand them as you did the rest of the bench. Also sand any other unsanded parts near joints. To sand interior corners, fold small sheets of sandpaper and use them by hand.

Breaking the edges

The choice of edge treatment (see p. 136) should fit the use and aesthetic intent of a piece of furniture. A heavily rounded edge is user friendly but can seem informal to the point of slovenliness. A molded edge is often reminiscent of antique furniture. A sharp edge is formal and gives maximum definition to the lines of a design. In general, a crisper edge reveals more exacting craftsmanship.

For this bench, I prefer a slightly broken edge made with 180-grit paper and a sanding block. The edge can be chamfered or rounded. My intention is to have crisp lines without the coldness of a totally hard edge. Break the edges of your bench to the extent you desire. If sandpaper doesn't take off as much wood as you like, begin with a file.

Wetting the surface

At this point, the bench is fully formed in every detail, and all surfaces have been sanded with 150-grit or finer paper.

The abrasive action of sandpaper cuts off some fibers but crushes others down. Dampening the surface causes the crushed fibers to swell, making them more susceptible to the next sanding, much like those early television ads in which shaving cream made whiskers stand up.

Apply clean water to all surfaces of the bench with a rag, dampening the wood but not flooding it. Let the bench dry overnight.

Final sanding

Sand the entire bench with 220-grit paper. Sand with the grain and into corners as much as possible. An orbital sander will reach most of the surfaces, or you can do the entire job by hand, as I do. When sanding is complete, the bench is ready for finishing.

APPLYING THE FINISH

Finishes protect wood against dirt and liquids, provide a partial moisture barrier, and enhance wood's appearance. Of the many types of finish available (see the sidebar on pp. 147–149), my favorite for this project is an oil/varnish mixture, which combines some of the good points of each component. I prefer to mix my own formula, but there are similar products of good quality available commercially. (You can also experiment by developing your own mixture with whatever oils and varnishes are available.)

The recipe for my finish is one-third pure tung oil, one-third Waterlox Original (a brand of semigloss wiping varnish made from tung oil), and one-third mineral spirits. Stir well and, preferably, allow the mixture to sit overnight in a sealed jar to give the ingredients time to blend. Only three coats of this oil/varnish formula are required to build up a good finish. If you choose to finish your bench with it, the steps are as follows; if you make your own oil/varnish finish, the same steps apply.

STEP 1 First coat.

When the bench has been finish-sanded with 220-grit paper, dust it off with an air hose and/or rags. Put on latex or vinyl gloves, and apply the first coat of finish with a small, clean, cotton rag. Cover all surfaces liberally, and keep them wet for five to ten minutes so plenty of oil can soak in. Wipe the surface dry with clean cotton rags before the finish gets tacky. Dispose of oily rags properly.

There may be some bleed-out, but it won't last more than 45 minutes. Give the bench a rubdown every five to ten minutes until finish stops migrating to the surface. It is important that no finish remains on

CAUTION

Oily rags may spontaneously combust if left in a clump or balled up. As soon as you are finished with a rag, spread it flat to dry or place it in a lidded metal can made for disposal of flammable materials.

There are many finishes, each of which has strengths and weaknesses. They vary in ease of application, water resistance, solvent resistance, dirt resistance, surface buildup, gloss, durability, toxicity, and ease of repair. The most commonly used finishes are oils, varnish and urethane, oil/varnish mixtures, wax, wiping varnishes, shellac, and lacquers.

Oils

Two types of oil are used for finishing furniture: linseed oil, which is pressed from flax seed, and tung oil, which comes from the nut of the tung tree. Though tung oil originated in China, much of it is now imported from South America. Tung oil is superior to linseed oil, with greater water resistance and less tendency to darken over time.

In their pure forms, these oils dry slowly and stay relatively soft. To make them dry faster and harder, they are often treated with heat and/or additives in the manufacturing process. Treated linseed oil is called "boiled" linseed oil. The advantages of oil finishes are:

■ **Ease of application.** You just put some oil on the wood with a rag, let it soak in, and wipe off the excess.

■ **Appearance.** Properly applied oil finishes dry in the wood, rather than on top of it. The absence of surface buildup gives the wood a visual and tactile immediacy that most other finishes lack.

■ **Ease of repair.** Stains and scratches can be sanded out and re-oiled without stripping the entire surface. However, most woods change color because of oxidation or exposure to sunlight, so a freshly sanded spot remains a different color for quite a while.

The disadvantages of oil finishes are:

■ **Relatively little protection** against liquids, moisture, and scratches.

■ **Many coats are required** to develop a decent buildup.

■ **Wet oil can bleed** out of the pores for hours, making the finishing process tedious.

■ **Unless you stay on hand** to wipe the surface, bleed-out dries into shiny little spots.

Varnish and Urethane

Varnishes are surface coatings, traditionally made by cooking oil and resin together and combining the mixture with thinner (mineral spirits). Modern varnishes usually substitute synthetic alkyd resin for natural resins. Urethane is a varnish that contains some proportion of polyurethane resin instead of the normal alkyd resin.

Varnish is usually applied with a brush, dries much harder than oil,

(continued on p. 148)

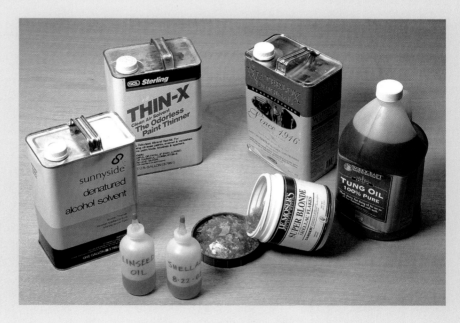

and takes a long time to dry. Excellent resistance to water, solvents, and moisture, as well as abrasion protection, makes varnish an ideal finish for marine and outdoor uses. On fine furniture, however, varnish creates too thick a surface film for my taste—the wood almost seems to be sealed in plastic.

Practice and care are required in applying varnish, which readily shows brush marks, traps air bubbles, and picks up dust.

Oil/Varnish Mixtures

Oil/varnish mixtures are applied like oil, but dry faster and harder, with fewer coats required to build up a good-looking finish. There is no appreciable surface coating to destroy the tactile quality of the wood. Although they are nowhere near as protective as straight varnish, oil/varnish mixtures definitely provide better moisture and liquid resistance than does oil alone.

Oil/varnish mixtures are at their greatest disadvantage as tabletop finishes because standing water penetrates them. The result can be discoloration of the finish and/or discoloration and change of texture in the wood. Water stains can often be repaired by rubbing with fine steel wool or wet-sanding with more finish after the seepage has dried.

I often use oil/varnish mixtures on tabletops, anyway. The wonderful appearance more than offsets the maintenance risks. A more protective finish would necessarily take the form of a thicker surface coating.

Wax

Wax is generally used as a coating over other finishes, rather than as a primary finish. It does not seal the wood, which is the primary job of any finish, nor does it offer much water resistance. Applied over another finish, however, wax can greatly enhance the appearance of the wood.

Common waxes used on furniture include paraffin, carnauba, and beeswax. Most commercially sold paste-wax finishes include one or more of these waxes, mixed with solvent to make them soft enough for easy application.

I do not put wax on my furniture. It is a high-maintenance finish that requires frequent repolishing. Just the warmth of a person's hand can soften wax enough to disrupt the surface.

Wiping Varnishes

Some of the "oil" and "tung oil" products sold to woodworkers are actually wiping varnishes—varnishes that have been thinned with a high proportion of mineral spirits. Moreover, some "tung oil" products

may not contain any tung oil, so read the labels carefully.

Wiping varnish can be applied with a rag like an oil finish or with a brush like varnish. Because it is so thin, though, wiping varnish doesn't build up enough film to allow for proper rubbing out and tends to look streaky and cheap as a surface coating.

Shellac

Shellac is made from a secretion of the lac beetle. It originated in the Orient and was long the premier finish for fine European furniture, but it has generally been replaced by more durable synthetic lacquers.

Shellac is brittle (as are varnish and lacquer). The fine crackling associated with antiques is shellac's response to the seasonal movement of wood. Shellac is also readily dissolved by alcohol and doesn't have good long-term water resistance.

Natural shellac has an orange tint that some furniture makers feel favorably warms up the appearance of dark woods. "Blond" shellac has been bleached clear and can be used on any wood.

Shellac is sold as dry flakes or premixed with alcohol. In liquid form, shellac has a short shelf life: It loses the ability to dry hard. Check the expiration date on the can when you buy premixed shellac. Making your own mixture from shellac flakes and alcohol avoids waste; you can mix just as much as you need.

With alcohol for a solvent, thin coats of shellac dry almost instantaneously. A technique known as padding takes advantage of this characteristic to build up a complete, lustrous finish in one sustained onslaught. A cotton rag, enclosing a wad of cotton material charged with shellac, is rubbed over wood with a continuous motion. As shellac builds up on the wood, drops of linseed oil are applied to offset the increased drag on the pad. The process concludes with long sweeps along the grain from end to end to avoid stop/start marks.

French polishing is a more sophisticated refinement of padding. A well-done French polish is an exquisite finish compared with varnish and spray lacquers, in the same way that fine crystal aces out glass and plastic.

Shellac can also be applied with a brush. It is sometimes used as an initial sealer prior to other finishing processes.

Lacquers

"Lacquer" describes a broad family of synthetic finishes. These include more traditional nitrocellulose-based lacquers and the newer water-based lacquers. Lacquer is generally applied with spray guns.

Like varnish and shellac, lacquer is a surface finish. The popularity of lacquer among professional furniture makers and manufacturers stems from the speed and control with which it can be applied and the ease with which gloss and tint can be varied.

Fillers

The pores of open-grained woods such as oak and mahogany tend to telegraph through a surface finish, especially in reflected light. Unless the pores are filled ahead of time, many layers of finish must be applied and sanded flat to fill them before surface buildup can begin.

Fillers are fine-grained pastes or powders that can be tinted to match the wood. They are used to fill open pores before applying finish. Traditionally, plaster of Paris was used to fill mahogany before French polishing. Nowadays, paste fillers are made from silica that has been mixed with a water-based or oil-based binder.

Filler is unnecessary when using an oil or oil/varnish mixture, since there is no surface buildup to highlight pores.

Padding with shellac.

the wood or in any interior corners. Let the bench dry overnight before going on to step 2.

On large pieces of furniture, it is advisable to oil and dry one section at a time to prevent the oil from setting up before there is time to wipe it off.

STEP 2 Second coat.

Hand-sand all surfaces with 400-grit sandpaper, always working with the grain. The purpose of this sanding is to smooth the surface finish, not to remove wood. Clean the dust off with a rag and apply the second coat of finish to one area of the bench at a time, such as the stretcher or the inside of a leg. Before the oil sets, wipe the surface dry and move on to another sec-

The completed bench.

tion of the bench. Remember to keep wiping with dry cotton rags every ten minutes or so until there is no more bleed-out. Dispose of oily rags properly.

Let the bench dry overnight before applying the final coat.

STEP 3 Final coat.

Repeat step 2, except this time sand with 600-grit sandpaper. Let the bench dry overnight.

The next day, examine the bench top in reflected light. If it looks at all streaky, try buffing the top under hard pressure with a clean rag. If it still looks streaky, lightly buff the entire surface with 0000 steel wool or a white nonwoven nylon abrasive pad (i.e., Scotch-Brite®), followed by a cotton rag, moving with the grain.

Congratulations! Your bench is now complete. Take it in the house and use it. Even if all the details aren't perfect, the bench is likely to be around for a lot longer than you and I. As with all fine furniture, it is best to keep it out of direct sunlight, which will bleach the wood. Likewise, avoid prolonged contact with water.

Now that you have made a piece of furniture from start to finish, it should be evident that good-quality work builds step by step. The attention given to each detail affects the integrity of the whole. With practice, your hands will come to understand the tools and your eyes will learn to discern the details that add up to successful results. Practice makes perfect, so let's move on to the next project.

PROJECT 5

Building a Side Table

O UR FINAL PROJECT, an Arts and Crafts–inspired table, expands upon the skills developed in the previous four projects. It introduces techniques essential to case-piece construction, such as door and drawer making, frame-and-panel construction, and web-frame construction. It also introduces new tools and methods, such as cutting mortises with a router and tenons with a table saw.

A relatively complex project like this is best approached one stage at a time. First, we'll construct the carcase (see pp. 153–173), then make the drawer to fit (see pp. 177–178), and, finally, make and mount the door (see pp. 179–182). Each stage is comprehensible on its own. To avoid repetition, instructions are based on the assumption that the reader has read and completed the previous projects in this book.

The scale plans on p. 152 are somewhat more complex than those I would make for myself. By necessity of the book format, they attempt to contain the complete information that I would normally include in a full-scale drawing. Feel free to alter the dimensions to suit your own needs and tastes and to draw your own full-scale plans.

SCALE DRAWING OF SIDE TABLE

Plan view of top showing shelf joinery

Plan view of web frame above the drawer opening

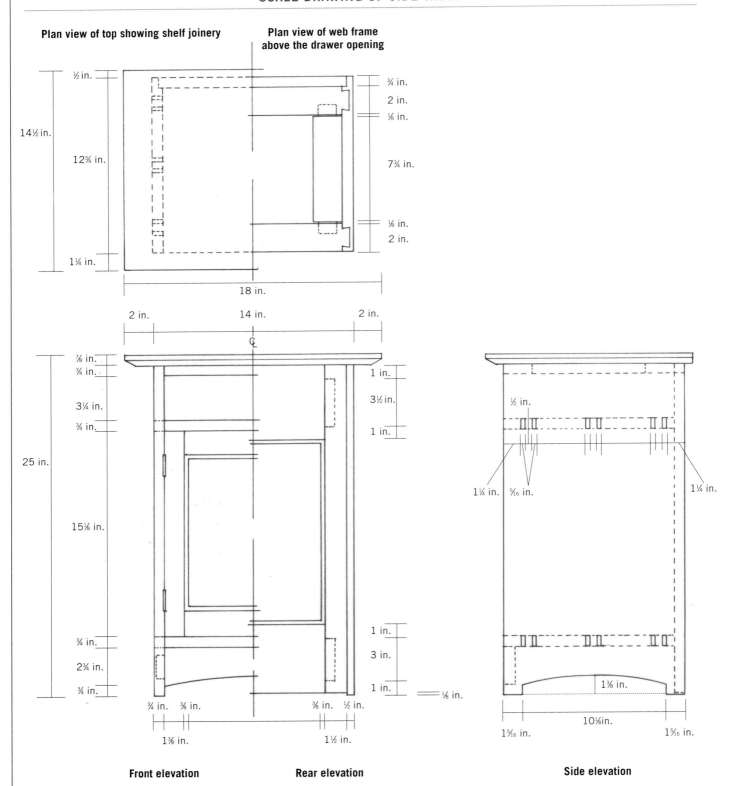

Front elevation

Rear elevation

Side elevation

What You'll Do

1. Make a cutting list.
2. Select the lumber.
3. Mill the wood.
4. Join the shelves to the sides.
5. Rout the rabbets for the back.
6. Cut the apron mortises.
7. Assemble the carcase for marking purposes.
8. Cut the apron tenons.
9. Fit the web-frame stiles.
10. Fit the web-frame rails.
11. Drill holes to fasten the top.
12. Take care of a few last details.
13. Glue the carcase together.
14. Clean up and sand.
15. Make the back.
16. Make the top.

BUILDING THE CARCASE

The carcase of the table is essentially a box created by joining the two shelves to the sides. Add to that a bottom apron, a frame-and-panel back, a drop-in web frame above the drawer, and the top, and the carcase is complete.

STEP 1 Make a cutting list.

If you intend to follow the plans in the scale drawing on the facing page, the cutting list for the carcase is as shown at right. In the previous project, the cutting list gave the exact finished dimensions of each piece. This project is a bit more involved and some of the cutting list dimen-sions, specifically those of the shelves, are larger than final size to facilitate the construction process.

Also, the cutting list gives the dimensions of the apron, top frame, and the back frame as they appear in the scale drawing, but in fact the sizes of these components will be taken from the exact dimensions of the actual carcase as it is constructed. In the meantime, you can mill these components to final thickness and width from the start but leave them up to 1 in. longer than indicated on the cutting list.

STEP 2 Select the lumber.

When possible, I prefer to make a project out of one large board or several boards from the same tree for the best possible match of grain and color throughout. Resawing a thick board is a good way to get a lot of wood out of a single timber. However, in building this piece, I was fortunate to have a 13-in.-wide, 10-ft.-long, clear

CUTTING LIST FOR CARCASE

☐ 2 pieces at ¾ in. x 12¾ in. x 24⅛ in. (the two sides)

☐ 2 pieces at ¾+ in. x 12¾ in. x 14 ⅛ in. (the shelves)

☐ 1 piece at ¾ in. x 2¾ in. x 13½ in. (the apron)

☐ 2 pieces at ¾ in. x 2 in. x 13½ in. (the web-frame stiles)

☐ 2 pieces at ¾ in. x 2 in. x 9½ in. (the web-frame rails)

4/4 cherry board to work with, which was just sufficient to provide all the parts that show as exterior surfaces. More often, particularly with larger projects, you end up combining unrelated boards, matching color and grain as best you can.

STEP 3 Mill the wood.

Mark out the components for the carcase on the rough lumber. This is always a balancing act between making the best use of attractive grain and efficient cutting to minimize waste. In order to stretch the wood from my chosen board to make all the visible surfaces of the table, I had to make the top shelf from another board and edge it with a strip from the preferred board.

The cutting list specifies the shelves at the same width as the sides, even though they will be ¾ in. narrower when the table

The author resaws a piece of 4/4 cherry for the door and back panels.

is complete. Starting with the shelves and sides at the same width makes it much easier to lay out precise joinery between them. To facilitate accuracy, cut the sides and shelves at the same time, using the same setting on the table saw. The shelves will be ripped to final width after the joinery is complete.

Also, the cutting list specifies that the shelves be milled to ¾+ in., which means just a hair thicker than ¾ in. This allows them to be planed down later to fit snugly into dadoes in the sides. Finally, the cutting list specifies the shelves ⅛₆ in. longer than final dimension so that the tenons at both ends will be ⅓₂ in. proud until they can be trimmed flush.

Mill the wood four-square to the specifications of your cutting list, allowing extra length as suggested in step 1. (For detailed directions on milling a board four-square, see pp. 77–92). If you are making the wide boards by edge-gluing narrow ones together, and if the full width is within the capacity of your thickness planer, then there are two distinct approaches to consider. One is to mill the wood to final thickness and then glue it. The other, which I prefer, is to mill the wood about ⅛₆ in. oversize in thickness and glue it together. After the glue dries, I can touch up one face of the assembly with a handplane, if necessary, to be sure it's flat, and then skim it to final thickness in the planer. This second method generally yields parts that are flatter and more stable.

There are two frame-and-panel constructions in this table, one for the door and one for the back. The panels are only

A BOOKMATCHED PANEL

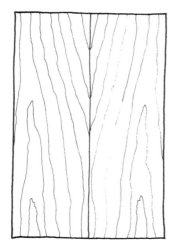

Bookmatching can create appealing grain configurations.

⅜ in. thick, and I have chosen to "book-match" both of them by resawing 4/4 stock and assembling the halves to form mirror images. Resawn wood often has movement problems because the inside and outside of the timber weren't at moisture equilibrium. It's a good idea to resaw early in the making process to allow the rough panels plenty of time to get all the kinks out and reach a new moisture equilibrium before they are milled to final thickness.

STEP 4 Join the shelves to the sides.

There are quite a few ways to join the shelves to the sides. One of the strongest, most durable, and best looking is the "Alan Peters joint" shown on p. 158, which I have used here.

Here are instructions for cutting the Alan Peters joint:

■ Make sure the carcase sides and shelves are cut to identical widths and consistent lengths.

■ Decide on the orientation of each piece and mark it boldly so that you know which is the front edge, which is the inside face, and which way is up.

■ Mark the locations of the dadoes across the inside faces of both carcase sides with a fine pencil and a square. Instead of measuring, which always carries the risk of error, it's good practice to transfer the dado locations directly from your full-scale drawing onto one of the sides and then transfer them directly from that piece onto the other.

■ Cut the dadoes. This can be done with a dado blade on the table saw, but I find a router preferable because it leaves a cleaner bottom surface. A simple, accurate way to guide the router is to build a little T-square jig, as shown in the drawing below. After you've made the jig, install a ¼-in. two-flute straight bit in the router, set it to cut at a depth of

A T-SQUARE JIG FOR THE ROUTER

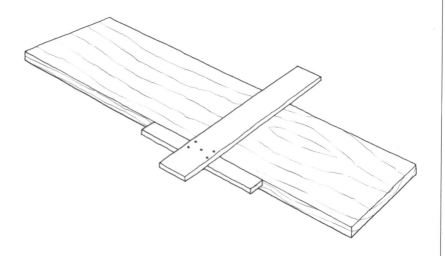

4

Rout the dado for the Alan Peters joint.

⅛ in., and make test cuts on a piece of scrap. The main purpose of the test is to leave cuts from the router bit in the fences on both sides of the jig. You can then match these cuts to the lines you have pencilled onto the work to orient the fence accurately. Be sure to clamp the fence and work firmly in place before routing.

Rout the dadoes, keeping the base of the router against the jig at all times. The direction in which you move the router is important. In one direction the cutting action of the bit helps to hold the router against the jig; in the other direction the bit pushes the router away.

ROUTER TIPS

When using a router and the T-square jig:

■ Be consistent in using the same side of the router base against the fence every time because the collet that holds the bit is not always truly centered.

■ The router bit can tear out the grain at the edges of the board. You can minimize this problem by moving the router slowly as it enters and leaves the wood. A more sophisticated method would be to back up the edge of the board with scrap material.

■ There are advantages to working with the fence against the front edge of the work, rather than the back edge. The first is that the fence serves as a backup board to prevent tearout on the edge where it really matters visually. The second is that, even if your T-square jig is a tiny bit out of square, your shelves will line up perfectly across the front of the piece and any deviation will be at the back.

The correct method is to move the router counter-clockwise "around" the jig, if you're looking down on it.

■ After the dadoes are cut, use a sharp pencil and a square to accurately mark their locations around to the other face of each piece.

■ Mill the shelves to final thickness so that they snugly fit the dadoes.

■ Cut the shelves to the length specified in the cutting list (see p. 153). Using a cutting gauge, mark the shoulders around each end. Allow for the tenons being ¹⁄₃₂ in. proud and the shoulders extending ⅛ in. into the dadoes.

■ Mark the locations of the mortises on both faces of the two side pieces and use the same gauge(s) at the same settings to mark the tenons on the shelves. Accurate, consistent marking is the secret to this joint. Because you have cut the sides and shelves to the identical widths, you can use both front and back edges as references. The outside pairs of mortise and tenons can be marked with a mortise gauge, but you'll need a cutting or marking gauge with a longer beam to mark the center pairs. (See the discussion on p. 133 for alternate marking methods.)

It is likely that the depth of the dadoes is greater than the length of the pins on your mortise gauge. If this is the case, the gauge will only scribe marks in the central portion of each dado. To extend those marks right up to the edges of the dado, I laid the blade of a square

Mark the mortises in the dadoes.

in the dado and marked across the end of it with an awl.

■ Cut the through mortises, following the same process as outlined on pp. 132–133.

■ Cut the tenons. This is essentially the same process we followed in project 2. First pare back to the shoulders in the waste areas between the tenons. Then saw the cheeks accurately, using either a dovetail saw or a bandsaw. Next, remove most of the waste from between the tenons with a coping saw or bandsaw. Finally, chop back precisely to the shoulders with a chisel.

■ Fit the joint. Eventually you will saw wedge kerfs in the tenons, but leave them whole for now so that they will be less susceptible to damage.

The complete parts of
the Alan Peters joint.

The joint assembled.

STEP 5 Rout the rabbets for the back.

Install a ¾-in., two-flute straight bit and an
edge guide on the router. The rabbets are
¼ in. deep and ¾ in. wide, so cut them
gradually, taking two or three passes at in-
crementally deeper settings. This will give
you a cleaner cut and reduce stress on the
router. The direction of feed should be
against the rotation of the bit (i.e., coun-
terclockwise in relationship to the work).

Set up a router to rabbet the table sides where they will accept the back.

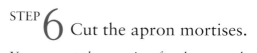

Routing the rabbet for the back frame.

You can use a plunge router with an edge guide to make the apron mortises.

STEP 6 Cut the apron mortises.

You can cut the mortises for the apron by the handwork methods that we introduced in project 2, or you can use a plunge router. To work with a router, install a

Square the ends of the mortises with a chisel.

6

7

Mark the shoulders of the apron directly from the assembled carcase.

¼-in. upcut spiral bit and an edge guide. Set the depth of cut to ¾ in. and align the edge guide to put the bit directly over the mortise location. The way I prefer to handle the router is to first plunge holes all the way to the bottom of the mortise at each end, then take out the waste in between with a series of shallow horizontal passes, penetrating about ⅛ in. deeper each time. Finally, I square the ends of the mortise with a ¼-in. chisel.

STEP 7 Assemble the carcase for marking purposes.

Clamp the shelves and sides together so that they pull tight and the carcase is square. This will allow you to mark the shoulders of the apron, the shoulders of the web-frame stiles, and the final depth of the shelves from reality. Place the clamps so they deliver pressure right across the shelves, not above or below where they would flex the sides. Hold the apron and stiles in place against the clamped carcase and use a knife to transfer their shoulder locations for an exact fit. Likewise, make accurate marks on the shelves to show where they meet the rabbets for the back.

STEP 8 Cut the apron tenons.

Once you've marked the shoulders of the apron directly from the assembled carcase, lay out the tenons. First, measure the length of each tenon beyond the shoulders, mark it, and crosscut the ends. To mark the cheeks, set the distance between the pins of your mortise gauge against the actual mortise made by the router (if that's what you used) and then set the gauge's fence to center the tenon on the apron.

Mark the ears and cut the tenons as explained in project 2 (see pp. 100-105).

An alternative method would be to cut the tenons on the table saw, as explained in the sidebar on pp. 162–163. But for just the one apron, I prefer the accuracy of marking the shoulders directly from the carcase and cutting them by hand to the iffy process of setting up the table saw to leave exactly the right shoulder span.

STEP 9 Fit the web-frame stiles.

Having marked the shoulders of the web-frame stiles directly from the carcase, measure out the lengths of the tails and cut the ends square. Then lay out the tails and cut them as explained in project 3.

After the tails are cut, lay the stiles in place on the carcase and trace the tails with a sharp pencil to mark the pins. Then cut the pins as described on pp. 112–113 and fit the joints. Note that here you are working to a pencil line instead of a cutting-gauge inscription for the depth of the pins.

STEP 10 Fit the web-frame rails.

Mark and cut the mortises and tenons that attach the web-frame rails to the stiles, following the same procedures used in project 2. The main thing to be aware of here is that we are purposely making the shoulders of the rails ⅛ in. short to allow for wood movement in the carcase.

This is a good place to try cutting mortises with a plunge router, as explained in the sidebar on pp. 166–167.

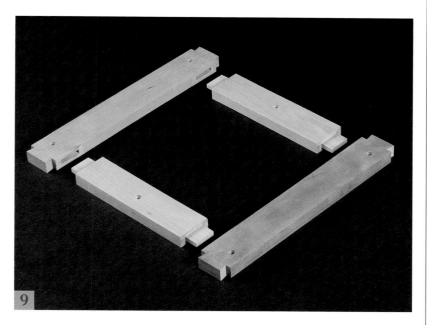

The component parts of the web frame.

STEP 11 Drill holes to fasten the top.

There are two sets of holes required. One set is countersunk in the underside of the web frame to accept the screws; the other is drilled through the upper shelf to allow access for the screwdriver.

The screws we will use are 1¼-in., #8, flat-head steel wood screws. Although brass screws are considered more refined in appearance, steel is preferable where it doesn't show because it is less likely to snap or strip.

Pull the web frame from the carcase and mark the locations of the holes on the underside—a hole at each end of each stile and a hole at the center of each rail. Make the holes just large enough to accept the full diameter of the screw shank and countersink them from underneath so the screw heads will be slightly inset rather than proud.

Making Tenons on the Table Saw

There are any number of ways to cut tenons with woodworking machines. What follows is a straightforward method of using the table saw for consistent, accurate results.

1 Make sure that all pieces that need to match, such as the rails of a door, are milled at the same settings to identical thickness, width, and length. The length should be the desired span between the shoulders plus the lengths of the tenons at each end. Ideally you would mill one or two extra pieces (perhaps of a less valuable timber) along with the rails, in order to test your setups as you go along.

Back the wood with a miter gauge to cut the shoulders.

2 Cut the shoulders. Set the rip fence so that the distance from the fence to the outside tips of the teeth that hook to the left is the desired tenon length. Set the height of the blade to the depth of the shoulder. You may have to change the height setting in process if the "ear" shoulders are different depths than the "cheek" shoulders.

With the miter gauge backing the work at all times and the end of the work against the rip fence, make the shoulder cuts. This method works perfectly if the vertical face of your rip fence is square to the table. When working with larger stock than we are here, fasten a wood fence to the miter gauge to lengthen it for added control and safety.

3 After the shoulders are cut, saw the cheeks with a fixture designed to hold the work securely upright. There are a number of designs available commercially, or you can make your own fixture such as the one shown in the top left photo on the facing page, which is designed to ride on the rip fence.

Set the height of the blade to just a hair less than the length of the tenon, clamp the work in the fixture, and set the fence so that the blade cuts the outside cheek. Make the

Saw the cheeks with the aid of an upright fixture.

Work against a fence on the bandsaw for a convenient way to trim the ears.

The completed tenon.

first pass, forward and back, then flip the wood and make a second pass for the other cheek. Usually you start off cutting the first tenon a shade thick, then home in on the right setting. Once the fence is set correctly, you can zip through the remaining tenons.

4 Cut the ears with a bandsaw. Working against a fence, as shown in the top photo at night, is optional.

To give a screwdriver access for assembly, drill ½-in.-dia. holes in the upper shelf directly below each of the screw holes in the apron.

STEP 12 Take care of a few last details.

The carcase joinery is now complete, but there are still a number of details to attend to before gluing it together. Some of these are obvious, but others, such as cutting the hinge mortises and installing the drawer stop, are things you might not think of the first time through.

- Cut the shelves to final width, so that they are flush with the rabbet at the back.

- Cut the wedge kerfs in the tenons.

- Make wedges from a contrasting wood.

- Mark, cut, and clean up the cutouts in the apron and sides.

- Scrape and sand interior surfaces, including the front and bottom of the apron (see pp. 138–139).

- Cut the hinge mortises in the carcase now, when they are fully accessible, rather than after it is glued, if you like, following the instructions on pp. 180–181.

- Make and install the drawer stop (see the bottom photo on p. 178). If you cut the stop a little wider than necessary now, it can be trimmed back later when fitting the drawer.

Carcase components ready for assembly.

12

STEP 13 Glue the carcase together.

Apply clamp pressure directly across the shelves and apron, rather than above or below where it could distort the case. Use wooden cauls to protect the work from clamp jaws or to distribute clamp pressure more effectively, as necessary. Be sure the case is square.

Once the shelves, sides, and apron are clamped together, attach in the web frame. Remember that the tenons are not glued into the mortises at all. Only the dovetail joints receive glue.

Finally, glue and insert the wedges.

STEP 14 Clean up and sand.

When the glue has had time to dry, plane the proud tenons flush, and scrape and sand the exterior of the case.

STEP 15 Make the back.

The back of the carcase is a frame and panel. There are two common ways to go about constructing the frame. The simpler is to cut the corner joints, then rout a stopped groove in the stiles and a through groove in the rails. The more sophisticated way is to make the groove first, running it all the way through the rails and the stiles with a table saw or a router. The grooves then determine the locations of the mortise cheeks, while the tenons are haunched to fill the grooves where they come through the ends of the stiles.

For this project we will use the simpler of the two methods, which is perfectly satisfactory for work of this scale.

The steps for making the back are as follows:

■ Make a cutting list. Build the frame about $\frac{1}{16}$ in. oversize in width so you can plane it to fit later, and about $\frac{1}{8}$ in. under the full height of the opening to allow clearance at the floor. Also, leave the stiles extra long until the joints are cut and fit. This helps avoid splitting the short grain at the ends of the mortises when cutting the joints.

Measurements for the back should be taken from the actual carcase, not the drawing that preceded it. If your carcase measurements were exactly true to the drawing on p. 152, the cutting list for the back would read as shown at below.

■ Select and mill the lumber. The grain pattern of rails and stiles can give a frame aesthetic appeal. On the other

---

CUTTING LIST FOR BACK FRAME

☐ 2 pieces $\frac{3}{4}$ in. x $1\frac{1}{2}$ in. x 24 in. (stiles)

☐ 1 piece $\frac{3}{4}$ in. x $5\frac{1}{2}$ in. x 11 in. (top rail)

☐ 1 piece $\frac{3}{4}$ in. x 5 in. x 11 in. (bottom rail)

☐ 1 piece $\frac{3}{8}$ in. x 10 in. x 14 in. (panel)

MORTISING WITH A PLUNGE ROUTER

One alternative to hand-cutting mortises is to use a plunge router and a simple mortising box. A plunge router is designed so the motor can be moved up and down through the base while running, effectively raising and lowering the cutter. Adjustable stops determine the depth of penetration.

1 Install an upcut spiral bit in the router, of the same diameter as the mortise.

2 Mark the mortise on the work.

3 Place the work in the mortising box, supported on a piece of scrap so that the edge to be mortised falls just below the lip of the box. Hold the work in place with clamps or wedges. Also, make sure the box itself is firmly anchored with clamps or between bench dogs.

MORTISING BOX

¾ in.

5 in.

1½ in.

5 in.

20 in.

The dimensions given are those of the mortising box shown in the photos.

The mortising box must be deep and wide enough to hold the workpiece and narrow enough that the router base can span the top.

3

Wedge the workpiece in the mortising box with its top edge just below the lip.

With the edge guide against the outside of the box, rout the mortise in a series of passes, lowering the bit ⅛ in. at each pass.

6

4 With the machine off, lower the cutter until it just touches the surface of the wood. Set the depth stop to the desired length of travel beyond that point into the wood. Then raise the bit back through the base.

5 Set the router's edge guide against the outside of the mortising box to locate the bit directly over the mortise.

6 Rout the mortise as we did on pp. 159–160, drilling down at both ends before taking out the center in gradual sweeps.

7 For a perfectly centered mortise, turn the work around in the box and take another full-depth pass all the way through. (A centered mortise often becomes desirable when you are going to cut the tenons with machinery, as opposed to hand tools.)

8 Square the ends of the mortise with a chisel. (The alternative is to round the tenons with a file.)

Note that for routing repeat mortises you can nail stops across the top of the box to limit the travel of the router bit within the confines of the mortise. If you then mark the location of the first mortise on the inside of the box and set up the subsequent mortises in exactly the same place, the stops will work for all of them.

GRAIN PATTERN ON A FRAME

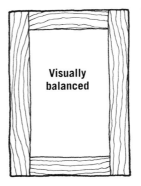 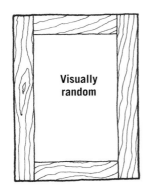

Visually balanced

Visually random

MORTISE-AND-TENON PROPORTIONS FOR UPPER RAIL OF BACK FENCE

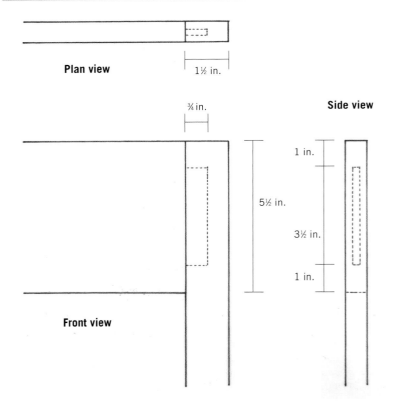

Plan view

1½ in.

¾ in.

Side view

Front view

1 in.

5½ in.

3½ in.

1 in.

hand, carelessly selected grain will detract from its appearance. The top drawing at left shows two different grain configurations for a frame. I find the balanced arrangement more attractive because the grain pattern of the rails and stiles relates to the space enclosed within.

The panel will be the most visually prominent feature of the assemblage, so pick a particularly attractive piece of wood or consider bookmatching, as I have done here.

After the frame components have been milled, mark their fronts so all the joinery can be laid out and cut from the same face.

■ Join the frame together with simple mortise-and-tenon joinery. Following the rules of tenon proportion established in project 2, I sized my tenons as shown in the bottom drawing at left. Note that the width of the tenon would be limited by its intersection with the panel groove (see the top drawing on the facing page).

Begin by laying out the mortises on one stile. First, mark the desired overall length of the stile. Leave extra wood at each end to be trimmed off later. Next, measure in from each end to locate the mortises. When the mortise locations have been laid out on one stile, transfer the marks directly to the other stile and scribe the mortise thicknesses with a mortise gauge. Once they are marked, you can cut the mortises by hand or with a router.

The tenons can be cut by hand or on the table saw. If by hand, first mark them out on one piece, then transfer the marks to the other. The distance between the shoulders plus the combined widths of the stiles should add up to the intended width of the frame (including that extra $\frac{1}{16}$ in.).

■ Rout through grooves in the rails and stopped grooves in the stiles. The scale drawing on p. 152 calls for grooves $\frac{1}{4}$ in. wide by $\frac{3}{8}$ in. deep. The stopped grooves should extend $\frac{3}{8}$ in. beyond the inside corners of the frame to accommodate the panel.

There are many ways to set up for this process with a router. The method I've used here is to set up a fence on a router table (see the sidebar on p.170). To cut the stopped grooves on a router table, you carefully drop the work down onto the bit, slide the wood along, and lift it off again where the cut stops. Another good method is to use a router box.

Whichever method you choose, there will be too much resistance to cut the groove at full depth on the first pass. Instead, take it in two or three steps, removing $\frac{1}{8}$ in. to $\frac{3}{16}$ in. at a time.

■ Complete the panel by gluing the halves together if that hasn't been done yet, then milling it to final thickness and dimension. The panel's width should allow about $\frac{1}{8}$-in. clearance in each groove for expansion. Even though the height of the panel does not have to allow for wood movement, you might leave the same amount of clearance top and bottom as you have on the sides so that the raised field is spaced consistently within the frame.

There are several options for thinning the edges of the $\frac{3}{8}$-in.-thick panel so they

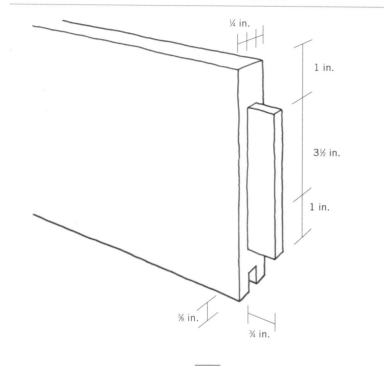

TENON FOR BACK FRAME

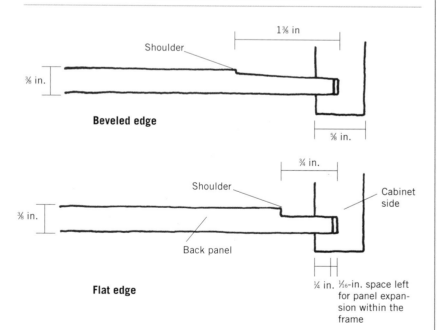

PANEL EDGE TREATMENTS

Beveled edge

Flat edge

Routing Grooves on a Router Table

Router tables are useful for routing through grooves in the rails and stopped grooves in the stiles, but they must be used with care. Keep a firm grip on the work at all times, particularly when lowering it onto a moving bit, as we are doing here.

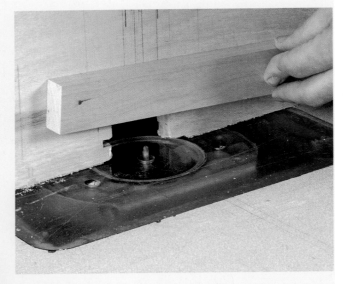

2 Begin the stopped stile grooves by carefully lowering the work onto the bit; finish by lifting the work where the cut stops.

1 The grooves in the rails can be routed straight through.

3 The completed panel grooves.

fit into the ¼-in. groove. Most
commonly, a flat or beveled edge comes
to a shoulder, as shown in the bottom
drawing on p. 169. Either version can
be cut on a table saw. Generally, the
shoulder is sawn first and the thickness
second (unless one vertical saw cut will
do the whole job). The shoulders should
be cut deep enough to prevent them
from pushing against the frame when
the panel expands. Make whichever
panel design you prefer. I like the
straightforwardness of a flat edge for
this piece.

After fitting the panel to the frame,
scrape and sand the panel. It is easier to
prepare the panel and the inside edges of
the frame for finishing now, rather than
after assembly. In fact, it is a good idea
to prefinish the panel at this point, for
two reasons. First, it is more accessible
now. Second, finish prevents any glue
that infiltrates the groove at the corner
joints from adhering to the panel.

■ Glue the frame and panel together. But
first, put a couple of ⅛-in.-thick spacers
in the bottom of the lower groove so
that the panel will be evenly spaced top
to bottom when installed. Spread glue
neatly on the cheeks of the mortises and
tenons so that it doesn't slop over into
the grooves.

■ Saw off the extra length at the ends of
the stiles. Then anchor the panel with
brads so it is centered between the stiles.
Predrill tiny holes (you'll need a wire-
sized bit smaller than ¹⁄₁₆ in.) so that you
can drive one brad in at the top center
and one at the bottom center. If you

**When making a raised panel, use a modified push
stick and a high auxiliary fence for safety. A
featherboard holds the panel against the fence.**

The cabinet back, ready for assembly.

don't have a countersink small enough, sink them with a small nail.

■ Fit the frame in the rabbets between the sides of the carcase with a handplane or by taking light passes on the jointer. Leave a little play to account for expansion of the stiles in humid weather. Also, clean up the ends of the panel with a plane, if necessary. Finally, plane the faces of the rails and stiles flush where they meet at the corners, as needed. Then scrape and sand the frames.

■ Screw the back to the shelves, through the stiles, with countersunk 1½-in. #8 flat-head brass wood screws. (I usually drive a steel screw of the same size into the hole first to pave the way for the softer brass.) Then remove the back so that you can more easily fit the drawer

and door and finish the inside of the carcase, all of which are yet to come.

STEP 16 Make the top.

Mill the pieces for the top to final thickness, edge-joint them, and glue them. Using a biscuit joiner or doweling jig to align the boards is good practice but not required so long as you are careful to avoid slippage. When the glue is dry, trim the top to final width and length.

Place the carcase upside down on the underside of the top, just where it belongs. Center the rails in the web frame so that the gaps at their shoulders are equal at both ends and mark the locations of the screw holes. Then remove the carcase and drill the screw holes in the underside of the top, making sure you don't pierce

One way to cut the bevels on the underside of the top is to use a table saw fitted with a high auxiliary fence.

16

What You'll Do

1. Select material and cut the drawer components to size.
2. Mark and saw the dovetails.
3. Cut the grooves for the bottom.
4. Cut the drawer bottom to fit.
5. Scrape and sand.
6. Prefinish the bottom.
7. Glue the drawer together.
8. Plane the drawer to fit.
9. Make and attach the pull.
10. Sand and finish the drawer.
11. Attach the drawer bottom.
12. Put in the drawer stop.

The drawer front should fit the opening tightly.

through to the other side. These holes should be about the same diameter as the solid shanks within the screw threads, so that only the thread will bite.

The bevels on the underside of the top can easily be put on with a handplane or they can be cut on the table saw and finished with a plane. If you use the table saw, attach a secure, tall auxiliary fence as shown in the photo on the facing page and concentrate on keeping the work against the fence for safety.

BUILDING THE DRAWER

You probably won't be surprised to learn that there are many ways to make drawers. In this case, we are going to make a traditional slip-bottom drawer with dovetailed corners. The process I prefer follows. Note that the drawer back is re-

cessed ⅛ in. below the top of the drawer. This makes it easier to plane the sides to fit during construction and, later, if they bind in response to humidity.

STEP **1** Select material and cut the drawer components to size.

Drawer sides are best made out of quartersawn wood to minimize expansion across the grain, but it's not an absolute necessity for a drawer this small.

Trim the drawer front so that it fits snugly into the front of the drawer opening on all sides, without play or gaps. This may require some handplaning, particularly if the opening isn't perfectly square. Trim the drawer back, which is ⅛ in. narrower, so it, too, fits the drawer opening snugly at both ends. Then trim the drawer sides so they slip in and out of the opening without getting stuck but without play. The length of the sides should be such that

CUTTING LIST FOR DRAWER

- ☐ 1 piece ⅝ in. x 3¼ in.
  x 12½ in. (drawer front)

- ☐ 1 piece ½ in. x 3⅛ in.
  x 12½ in. (drawer back)

- ☐ 2 pieces ½ in. x 3¼ in.
  x 11½ in. (drawer sides)

- ☐ 1 piece ⅜ in. x 11½ in.
  x 12 in. (drawer bottom)

the drawer ends up about ¼ in. shy of the full depth of the opening.

If the measurements of the drawer opening were exactly true to the drawing below, the cutting list would be as shown at left.

STEP 2 Mark and saw the dovetails.

I have chosen to make half-blind dovetails at the front of the drawer and through dovetails at the back. There are several special considerations in laying out these dovetails.

SCALE DRAWING OF DRAWER

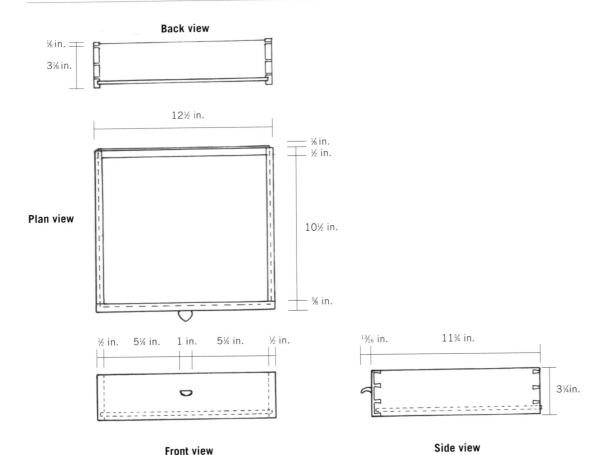

Back view

⅛ in.

3⅛ in.

12½ in.

⅛ in.
½ in.

Plan view

10½ in.

⅝ in.

½ in. 5¼ in. 1 in. 5¼ in. ½ in.

Front view

¹³⁄₁₆ in. 11¾ in.

3¼ in.

Side view

DRAWER-SIDE DOVETAIL LAYOUT

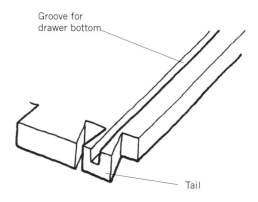

Groove for
drawer bottom

Tail

Generally, half-blind drawer dovetails should be laid out so that the bottom groove runs through a tail, rather than a pin. This allows the groove to be cut all the way through, instead of stopped.

First, at the drawer front, the layout of the dovetails should take into account the location of the groove for the drawer bottom. Construction is simpler if the groove falls entirely within the last tail, avoiding the pins wholly (see the drawing above). This allows you to cut the groove completely through each component and yet have it remain invisible from the outside.

Second, the dovetail joints at the drawer back should start and end with half-tails instead of half-pins. Otherwise you will see gaps in the rear corners of the drawer sides when the drawer is complete.

Third, when marking the shoulders for the pins, front and back, set your cutting gauge to the exact thickness of the sides. This makes the drawer sides flush with the front and back, which are already sized to fit the drawer opening perfectly. After assembly, the sides only require a few licks with a plane to slide in and out with a "piston fit."

When the dovetails are complete, dry-assemble the drawer and plane its bottom edges flush.

STEP 3 Cut the grooves for the bottom.

The grooves for the drawer bottom are drawn to be ¼ in. wide by ¼ in. deep. Cut them on the table saw, either with a dado blade or by making sequential passes with a single blade. Register the bottom edge of each piece against the fence for consistency.

The sequence is to cut the grooves in the front and sides first. Then raise the blade height so that you cut all the way through the back of the drawer. This leaves the back at the correct width so it will sit on top of the drawer bottom.

STEP 4 Cut the drawer bottom to fit.

The grain should run across the drawer, rather than front to back. The length should be about ¹⁄₁₆ in. less than the total distance between the groove interiors. The width should be such that, when fully inserted, the drawer bottom sticks out about ⅛ in. beyond the back.

The bottom of a larger drawer might be screwed to the back through slots that allow for wood movement, but that isn't necessary here.

STEP 5 Scrape and sand.

Scrape and sand the interiors of the drawer components and both sides of the bottom panel. Stay away from the joints. (For a detailed discussion of scraping and sanding, see pp. 138–139.)

STEP 6 Prefinish the bottom.

This is a good point at which to put the first coat of finish on the drawer bottom. I used shellac on this piece.

STEP 7 Glue the drawer together.

Dry-clamp, cut cauls, and glue the dovetails. To keep the assembly square, clamp the drawer bottom in place. Because it is prefinished, the bottom shouldn't stick, even if some glue infiltrates the grooves from the corners. (For a detailed discussion of gluing and assembly, see pp. 142–144.)

STEP 8 Plane the drawer to fit.

Plane the sides and edges of the drawer, as needed. At the most humid time of year, the drawer should ride freely in and out of the opening, without play from side to side or up and down. If you are working in the dry of winter, allow some play in the height of the drawer for seasonal expansion.

STEP 9 Make and attach the pull.

For directions on making the pull, see the sidebar on the facing page.

STEP 10 Sand and finish the drawer.

This is most easily done with the bottom removed.

STEP 11 Attach the drawer bottom.

Shove the bottom all the way into the front groove. A small brad through a predrilled hole in the bottom of the

The drawer components with dovetails and grooves cut, ready to glue.

MAKING DRAWER AND DOOR PULLS

The pulls should be pleasing to both the eye and the hand. They are not only visually important but also are the parts of the cabinet you touch. The drawing below shows the pull I designed for the door and the drawer. Pulls are often made of a contrasting wood—I chose ebony to contrast with the cherry of the carcase.

Before making the pulls, cut the mortises for them in the door stile and drawer front. Next, mill a piece of wood to the thickness and width of each pull, but leave it a couple of inches longer to make handling easy while cutting the tenon. When the tenon fits, cut the pull to length. Then carve, rasp, and/or file it to the shape you want. Finally, sand the pull and glue it in place.

DOOR-PULL DESIGN

Plan view

¼ in. ½ in. ¼ in.

½ in.

1³⁄₁₆ in.

Front view

Side view

⁷⁄₁₆ in.

⅛ in.
¼ in.
¹⁄₁₆ in.

The drawer pull is attached with a mortise-and-tenon joint.

The completed drawer.

The drawer stop in place.

drawer front, at the center, should be sufficient to hold it there so that all wood movement takes place toward the rear.

STEP 12 Put in the drawer stop.

Once the drawer fits, screw a small strip of wood inside the carcase, just behind the center of the drawer front, to serve as a

stop. If you have already made an extra-wide stop, as suggested on p. 165, this is the time to plane it to size. Fully closed, the front of the drawer should be flush with the front of the carcase.

BUILDING THE DOOR

The frame-and-panel door utilizes the same construction techniques as did the back of the carcase, so the construction process should be familiar up to the point where you install the hinges, catch, and pull.

STEP 1 Cut the door components to size.

Measure the assembled carcase to determine the exact size of the door opening. Build the door about ¹⁄₁₆ in. larger in both dimensions to provide leeway for irregularities such as the carcase being slightly out of square. If the measurements of the door opening were exactly true to the drawing on p. 152, the cutting list would be as shown above.

STEP 2 Construct the door.

Construct the door just as you did the back, right up to the point where you would begin to scrape and sand the frame after assembly.

CABINET HINGES

Butt hinge	Knife hinge	Invisible hinge

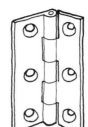  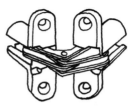

STEP 3 Plane the door to fit the opening.

Before scraping and sanding the assembled door, plane the top, bottom, and sides so that it fits the opening with scarcely any play.

STEP 4 Install the hinges.

This design calls for the traditional favorite, brass butt hinges. Butt hinges vary in quality. Some are pure brass while others are plated; some are well machined, with tight pins, while others are stamped, with loose pins and sloppier movements. The leaves of some are quite thin; others are thick and sturdy. Generally, the best hinges are available at woodworkers' specialty stores and through catalogs,

What You'll Do

1. Cut the door components to size.
2. Construct the door.
3. Plane the door to fit the opening.
4. Install the hinges.
5. Make the pull.
6. Install a door catch.

Use a marking gauge to scribe the distance the hinge is inset on the carcase.

The hinge mortise can be cut with a router or a chisel. Here the author uses a small router called a laminate trimmer.

but good ones can also be found at local hardware stores.

Select hinges that are sized appropriately to the scale of the piece. Butt-hinge measurements are given as length by open width. The hinges should not be so wide that their leaves extend beyond the inside edge of the door. Since the door is ¾ in. thick, the open width of the hinges should be no more than 1½ in. wide. Because the hinges I chose measure 1½ in. long by

1¼ in. wide, the hinge mortise will only partially span the thickness of the door.

Before mounting the hinges, determine the side on which the door will open.

To mount hinges:

■ With a pencil, mark the location of the hinges on the carcase at whatever distance from the top and bottom seems pleasing. If the mortises aren't set in far enough to give access to a router or laminate trimmer, you can cut the hinge mortise entirely with chisels.

■ Set a marking gauge to a hair less than the distance from the outside edge of a hinge leaf to the center of the hinge pin. Use the gauge to scribe the distance each hinge is inset from the front of the carcase.

■ Mark the exact ends of the hinge mortises with knife lines squared across the inside of the carcase.

■ Pare back to the knife lines from the waste sides.

■ Make the hinge mortises a hair deeper than the hinge leaf is thick. Waste can be removed with a router or a chisel. If you use a chisel, scribe the depth of the mortise with a marking gauge so you have a line to work to. If you use a router, set the depth of the cutter to a little more than the thickness of a hinge leaf. A fairly small (¼-in.-dia. or ⅜-in.-dia.) straight bit lets you rout close to the corners. You can use the router freehand, but be careful not to rout all the way up to the boundaries of the mortise; clean out the waste around the edges with a chisel.

- Place the door in the carcase and transfer the hinge-location marks to it.

- Repeat steps 2 through 5 to make hinge mortises in the door.

- Lay a hinge in each mortise, and mark a pilot hole at the center of every screw hole with an awl. Drill holes slightly smaller than the diameter of the screws. The prepackaged screws that come with hinges are often cheaply made, with threads cut all the way to the head, and the heads tend to snap off. Discard these and buy wood screws that have solid shanks below the head.

- Temporarily mount the hinges to the carcase and the door. (It helps to use steel screws that are the same size as the brass finish screws so that you don't ruin the latter.) With the door mounted, try to close it. Note where it rubs, remove it from the hinges, and plane it down. Then remount and check again. When you're done, there should be no more than $\frac{1}{32}$ in. clearance all the way around.

STEP **5** Make the pull.

See the sidebar on p. 177.

STEP **6** Install a door catch.

Hang the door again in order to install the catch. Commercially available catches include magnetic, ball, and bullet catches, among others. For this situation, where the catch must also function as a stop, I have chosen a double ball catch (see the drawing at right).

The completed hinge mortises in the door and the carcase.

DOUBLE BALL CATCH

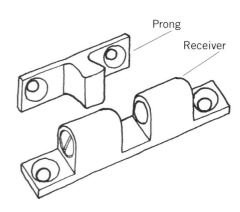

Prong

Receiver

There is no agreed-upon terminology, but we'll call the part of the catch that attaches to the carcase the "receiver" and the part that attaches to the door the "prong."

It is much easier to install the catch if you first remove the back from the carcase, so that you have access to the inside with the door closed. There is more than one good way to mount the catch, but the first steps for me are to decide at what height the catch will be located, assemble the catch, and hold it in position with the door closed. Next, I trace the screw holes

FINISHING THE TABLE

My preference, with most case pieces that have drawers or doors, is to finish the interior with shellac and the outside with an oil/varnish mixture. Although I generally prefer the appearance of oil/varnish, the odor of it hangs around an enclosed space for a long time. Shellac, on the other hand, dries quickly with a pleasant smell.

Finish shellacked surfaces first. Any spillover to exterior surfaces can easily be sanded off before applying the oil/varnish mixture. And any oil/varnish that gets onto a previously shellacked area can be wiped off without difficulty.

in the receiver onto the carcase interior with a sharp lead so I can drill pilot holes and screw the receiver in place.

To attach the prong to the door, I first insert it into the attached receiver (leaving about ½ in. of space between the edge of the prong and the backplate of the receiver bit to allow for the swing of the door). Next, I trace the screw holes in the prong onto the door, drill pilot holes, and screw the prong in place. Once the catch is installed, remove it and the hinges in preparation for sanding and finishing.

COMPLETING THE TABLE

The remaining steps are to scrape and sand all as-yet-unsanded surfaces and apply finish to all components. Then reinstall the hardware for the door, screw the drawer stop in place, screw on the top, and, finally, screw the back in place. The table is now complete and ready for a lifetime of enjoyment.

The completed table.

AFTERWORD

THIS BOOK OFFERS a solid grounding in the basics of woodworking. Having read it, you probably know what you would like to learn next and wonder how to go about it.

There is a wealth of information available through books, classes, and, most important, hands-on experience.

Through reading, you will discover that different authors suggest different ways of doing things. Remember, there is no one right way. With experience, you will develop methods of woodworking that are right for you—approaches that enhance your pleasure in the process and yield the results you are looking for.

Instruction is available through community colleges, degree programs, apprenticeships, workshop programs, and other schools. A good instructor is invalu-

able but not always easy to find. I particularly recommend workshops as a wonderful opportunity. Their intensive nature, along with the extensive interaction with faculty and other students, creates an atmosphere in which a tremendous amount of learning takes place.

In the long run, most learning comes through the experience of your own hands. Practice and observation are the two most reliable instructors in craftsmanship. I encourage you to design projects that extend your range of skills.

Above all, keep sight of the reasons you have chosen to pursue craftsmanship. The finished object is, at best, a reflection of the true rewards of the process—the personal sense of quality, joy, and integrity that comes from work well done.

INDEX

Index note: page references in **bold** indicate a drawing; page references in *italics* indicate a photograph.